ON A BUDGET

Emilie Barnes & *Yoli Brogger*

with

Anne Christian Buchanan

HARVEST HOUSE PUBLISHERS
Eugene, Oregon 97402

Cover by Garborg Design Works, Minneapolis, Minnesota

Cover illustration by Michal Sparks, copyright © Indigo Gate

DECORATING DREAMS ON A BUDGET
Copyright © 1999 Emilie Barnes and Yoli Brogger
Published by Harvest House Publishers
Eugene, Oregon 97402

Library of Congress Cataloging-in-Publication Data

Barnes, Emilie.
    Decorating dreams on a budget / Emilie Barnes and Yoli Brogger, with Anne Christian Buchanan.
      p. cm.
    Rev. ed. of: Beautiful home on a budget, c1998.
    ISBN 0-7369-0037-3
    1. Interior decorating—Handbooks, annuals, etc.   I. Brogger, Yoli.   II. Buchanan, Anne Christian.   III. Barnes, Emilie. Beautiful home on a budget.   IV. Title.
NK2115.B29
747—dc21   98-31157
                                                        CIP

Printed in the United States of America.

99 00 01 02 03 04 05 / LP / 10 9 8 7 6 5 4 3 2 1

Contents

Who We Are

And Why We Wrote This Book

NOTHING IS MORE FUN and more satisfying than the process of decorating your home—making it beautiful, making it "you," creating an inviting space that beckons family and guests alike. No time is better invested than the time you spend making your living space livable—not to mention comforting and warm and intriguing.

And yet nothing can be more frustrating than wanting a beautiful home but feeling inadequate—because money is tight, time is short, or just because "I'm not a decorator!" Maybe you love poring through decorating books or watching those great home improvement shows, yet you have trouble translating those great ideas to your real life. Maybe you're tired of living with your standard-issue drapes and ordinary chairs and sofas but you just don't know where to start doing things differently.

If any of those things is true of you (or if you just want to pick up some quick and easy ideas), we invite you to come on a decorating adventure with us. We want to load your imagination with simple, economical ideas for decorating your living space. We want to inspire you with how easy and fun it is to transform an ordinary room into a cozy, welcoming, distinctive one. And we want to encourage you to draw on your strengths, your personality, and your skills to make your home beautiful and unique, whether it's an estate or an apartment, owned or rented.

But first we'd like to tell you just a little about who we are and why we decided to write this book together.

The two of us are very different, though we share a love of beauty, a deep spiritual commitment, a sometimes offbeat sense of humor, and a passion for nest building. Emilie is organized and efficient; she teaches More Hours in My Day seminars and writes books on home organization and beautiful living. Before that she was a career homemaker. Her decorating strength is the ability to glean ideas from many different sources and put them to work in her own home. Emilie's tastes are classic and romantic with a country flavor. She is happiest when surrounded by antiques and quilts and gleaming English porcelain.

Yoli, on the other hand, is as impulsive as Emilie is organized. She is the "artistic type" who likes to live on the cutting edge of design, and she's bursting with creative ideas and energy. A professional designer who works in many different areas—from interior design to photo shoots to table settings—Yoli specializes in helping clients decorate their homes using furnishings and objects they already own. Her tastes are eclectic, ranging from the antique to the avant-garde, and her personal style tends toward elegantly "funky" (but always cozy and conversational).

Emilie's bedroom features Victorian prints and a four-poster bed.

Yoli's bedroom sports black-and-white stripes, English roses, and a straw hat in a frame.

Emilie decorates with ceramic roosters, folk art, and lots of silk flowers.

Yoli decorates with fabrics and classic collections as well as the newest of design accessories.

So why are we writing a home-decorating book together? Because we've been decorating friends forever, sharing advice, ideas, and afternoons at garage sales and swap meets. Because we've come to appreciate each other's strengths and to love one another's style. Because we think that the combination of our strengths and experience can give you some inspiration and ideas.

The point, after all, is not to show you how to decorate like Emilie or Yoli. The point is to learn to decorate like *you*—without breaking your back or your budget.

We'll show you ideas and techniques that are simple, fun, quick, easy, and economical—hoping we'll inspire your own ideas and get your own creative juices flowing.

This book is even designed to be quick and fun to read. It's written in short chapters that you can pick up while waiting on a carpool or enjoying your coffee break. Some chapters are how-to's, some are just ideas, a few are aimed at helping you explore your decorating dreams.

If we've done this book right, you'll be doing something new to your house before you even finish reading.

So let's get started—and have some fun.

—Emilie and Yoli

1

What's My Style?

Discovering Yourself as a Decorator

WHAT'S YOUR DECORATING STYLE? Before you
say "French country," "formal contemporary,"
"eclectic," or "Gee, I don't know"—you might want to
stop and think for a minute about what style is.

You see, decorating with style is not a matter of
putting a label on yourself. It's not a matter of following fashion or impressing people with your good
taste. Decorating with style is mostly a matter of being
yourself . . . but your most creative, expressive, beautiful self. It's a matter of taking your tastes, your personality, and your possessions and helping them show
their best face to the world. When you hit on the right
decorating style, your home will reflect more of who
you are—what you love, what activities you enjoy, how
you work, what brings you pleasure (as well as what
brings joy to your family).

Actually, you may already have a pretty good idea
of what your style is. After all, you've lived with yourself

awhile. You have a feel for what works for you and what doesn't. You have acquired some furniture, some accessories, some linens that you love (as well as a bunch of stuff you've acquired for a million other reasons). Those items you love are the place to start in decorating with style—but sometimes it's hard to get fresh ideas from familiar objects.

So even before you start looking at what you have, we suggest a little journey of self-discovery. You can do it in an afternoon or over the course of several months, and it's great fun.

The first thing you do is go shopping in all the places you can't afford. Seek out the scented gift shops, the exclusive department stores, the gleaming antique emporiums—all those places where you sometimes find yourself wistfully window shopping. You may even want to visit some model homes or show homes.

Don't think about cost on this particular shopping safari. Don't worry about whether a certain piece would fit your rooms or your lifestyle. Right now, just think about what you love. . . and why. Notice the woods, the fabrics, the color schemes, the room arrangements. Take notes. Make sketches. And don't worry about what people think. (They'll probably think you're a professional decorator!)

Then, on your way home, stop by a newsstand and buy a handful of decorating magazines. Try to get a variety—something country, something Victorian, something sleek and contemporary. Also pick up a gardening magazine or two, perhaps a fashion magazine, some "ladies' " magazines, or even something that covers celebrities. Buy some magazines you read regularly, some you never pick up. When you go to pay the bill for your stack of reading material, remind yourself of the price tags in the stores you just visited. A pile of magazines, believe us, is a bargain!

*Style is not what you have,
but what you do
with what you have.*

When you get home, the real fun begins. Pour yourself a refreshing cup of tea, find yourself a comfy corner, take your pile of magazines, and let 'er rip! Whenever you find something you like—a chair, a color scheme, a wall arrangement, a china pattern—tear it out. Don't stop to think too hard; just pull out whatever pages appeal to you and put them in a pile.

Yoli always does this when she acquires a new decorating client. She hands the new client a lapful of decorating magazines for a session of random ripping.

Once the client has collected a little pile of pictures, the two of them go through it together. By the time they're through, Yoli has a pretty good picture of that client's general tastes and style.

When you are through ripping, sort through your own stack of randomly ripped pages and try to get a general feel for why you chose the pages you did.

> *Why do we love certain houses,*
> *and why do they seem to love us?*
> *It is the warmth of our individual*
> *hearts reflected in our surroundings.*
>
> —T.H. Robsjohn Gibbings

Look for common elements—ambience, lighting, color schemes. Are you drawn to bare, sleek rooms or to cozy, cluttered looks? Do certain color schemes make you feel happy? Is your eye drawn by rustic folk art or gilt-framed Old Masters? Do you always end up tearing out florals . . . or plaids? What pages just make you want to step into them—and bring a friend?

As you answer these questions, you'll begin to get a picture of what your style really is. And that, of course, is the very best place to start.

Bright Ideas

Practical Considerations for
Beautiful Decorating

As you learn about your tastes and your style, here are some practical questions you should also ask yourself:

☼ *How often am I willing and able to clean house—and what kind of help is available? (If you despise dusting, does it really make sense to fill your house with dust-gathering knick-knacks?)*

☼ *Does the height, weight, or physical condition of anyone in my family affect my decorating choices? (Does somebody need oversized seating, lower cabinets, brighter lighting, or a clear floor with nothing underfoot? Is someone allergic to feathers, wool, or dust?)*

☼ *Do I need to consider the special needs of small children or pets? (Do sharp objects or houseplants need to be kept out of reach? Do feeding bowls or pet beds need to fit into the decorating scheme?)*

☼ *Will I do any work in this space that requires special equipment or lighting? (If you read a lot* or do crafts, you'll be smart to include space or lighting for these pursuits.)

☼ Do I need more storage? (Many decorating solutions can add significantly to your storage space.)

☼ Are there any particular decorating problems I need to solve? (An unsightly alcove, a stain on the ceiling, an awkward radiator can all be camouflaged with a little creative attention.)

☼ Do I expect to entertain often, and if so, how many people do I want to be able to accommodate at a time? (Consider table size, conversational groupings, and flow between dining and seating areas.)

2

Love What You Have

Treasure Hunting in Your Own Home

WHEN YOU DECORATE, you're not starting from scratch.

Few of us begin our decorating adventure with bare walls and an unlimited budget. In fact, many of us begin with cluttered rooms, limited funds, or both. Most of us have furniture or accessories of some kind—whether it's an "early married" accumulation, a college-apartment legacy, a "kid years" collection, or a "matched set" from 30 years ago.

Wherever you're starting—that's the place to start! The key to affordable decorating is creative seeing: learning to see new possibilities in your old stuff, beautiful uses for your ordinary stuff, and easy transformations for stuff you like but don't know what to do with.

It's probably the single most important key for home decorating on a budget: "Love what you have."

Loving what you have is a decision; it's a choice. It's very close to learning to love and accept yourself—a critical step in personal wholeness. It's also a positive decorating attitude that can transform your home and your life.

We've both come to realize over the years that people really don't recognize what treasures they have. So before you go out shopping for furniture and accessories, try a little attitude adjustment. Try going on a treasure hunt in your own home.

Start by clearing the center of a room, putting down a blanket, and sitting on it. Then empty out the cupboards, especially the ones where you store away the things you don't use. Put all that junk on the blanket. Pick up one thing at a time and ask yourself:

Am I drawn to this item? Does it have sentimental or emotional value to me? Do I find this beautiful or interesting? Is there some way I can use it creatively to decorate my home?

If the answer is no to all those questions, then that object may be ready for the garbage, the charity box, or the garage sale.

But if any of your answers is yes, the next questions are simply how-to ones—and that's where creative seeing comes in.

Say, for example, that you have a couple of pieces of Depression glassware that you kept from your grandmother's house, even though you really didn't think it fit your house. Maybe one could hold a bouquet of flowers or a votive candle in the bathroom—or perhaps the various pieces could be stationed around a bedroom as a motif. A stray cup and saucer could be filled with potpourri and perched atop a stack of old books next to an old pair of eyeglasses. Your little beaded evening bags could be arranged above a door or framed in a shadow box.

Most of us have acquired a sizable collection of baskets. Such a collection could look wonderful hanging from a ceiling (Emilie does this in her dining room), gathered atop a sideboard (Yoli does this), clustered under a library table, or hung from a wall in the garage. Large baskets can serve as magazine racks, hold onions in a dark corner, or even gather dirty clothes. Smaller ones can hold flatware, fruit, napkins, or correspondence.

Once you've gotten used to thinking "Do I like?" and "Can I use?" your treasure hunt can extend to the other rooms. Look for items that can be put to use in other ways or transformed with paint, glue, or other simple tools. Look for interesting items that could be framed or simply displayed on a wall as they are. Consider new ways to use tassels, hooks, drawer pulls, even costume jewelry. And be alert for collections you didn't know you had—like items that could make a statement if displayed as a group.

You might be surprised what close-to-home treasures you may find.

And then, once you've examined your own hidden treasure, you can begin to roam farther afield. (But that's a different chapter!)

Bright Ideas

The Art of Creative Seeing

All it takes is a bit of ingenuity to discover wonderful decorating possibilities in your familiar old possessions (or somebody else's old stuff). Here are some ideas for loving what you have:

- ✿ *A glassed-in bookcase can hold knickknacks in the bathroom.*

- ✿ *Any old furniture can be painted, refinished, or covered.*

- ✿ *An old sideboard can store sweaters in a bedroom.*

- ✿ *Tassels, ribbons, buttons, old jewelry can decorate almost anything.*

- ✿ *Rusty TV trays can be painted or decoupaged.*

- ✿ *A lingerie chest can store tapes and CDs.*

- ✿ *Baskets can be painted, threaded with yarn, or used as is.*

- ✿ *A magazine rack or old wastebasket can keep sheet music close at hand.*

- ✿ *A rusty mailbox can be scraped and painted or decoupaged.*

- ❀ A single chair can become a bedside table or a sofa table.

- ❀ Cardboard boxes can be covered with fabric and used for storage.

- ❀ A child's wagon can become a planter.

- ❀ A footstool or ottoman can be painted, padded, draped.

- ❀ Garden furniture can serve as house furniture.

- ❀ House furniture can serve as garden furniture.

- ❀ A moth-eaten chair can be slipcovered or reupholstered.

- ❀ Drawers from a broken desk can serve as trays.

- ❀ Small drawers can hold plants or spice jars.

- ❀ Old clothes can become pillows, place mats, etc.

- ❀ Tea towels or tablecloths can become curtains or valances.

- ❀ Almost anything can become a lamp—including an old lamp!

- ❀ A cracked pitcher or teapot can serve as a planter.

- ✿ An odd plate, bowl, or tray can decorate a wall or hold a planter.

- ✿ A crystal salt-shaker can hold a miniature bouquet on a nightstand.

- ✿ A stepladder can hold shelves or display family photos.

- ✿ A collection of flowerpots can hold candles or potpourri.

- ✿ Fabric remnants can be pieced together as patchwork.

3

The Rules and How to Break Them

Freeing Yourself from the "Shoulds"

FIRST OF ALL, THERE REALLY aren't any rules! That is, the decorating police will not arrest you for making a mistake in your decor. The neighbors might talk if you painted the whole house orange, and the authorities might object to a fire hazard. But most of us aren't in danger of these extremes. What we want are a few basic guidelines for tasteful and inexpensive decorating. Here are a few we think are helpful, plus a few common assumptions we'd like to challenge.

The Rules

RULE #1: Always think hospitable, comfortable, and cozy.

After that can come fashionable, sleek, dramatic, or whatever pleases you. But always keep in mind that a beautifully decorated home still has to function as a home!

RULE #2: Decorate for your family first.

Strive for a home that is truly welcoming to the people who live there. Your husband should not have to perch in chairs that feel too small. Your children should not have to avoid certain rooms. Consider every family member's comfort and taste when making decorating decisions. And don't fool yourself about how your family lives! If your husband watches TV a lot, don't hide the set under a side table.

RULE #3: Buy what you love—but avoid paying retail!

The fact is that you don't have to spend a lot to get a rich, fabulous look. Before you pay retail for anything, try garage sales, flea markets, discount stores, sales, and your grandmother's attic. Full price should be your last resort.

RULE #4: You don't always have to love what you buy if it works.

This is an important corollary to Rule #3. That is, if a certain side table fills a decorating need (fits that empty corner, makes an interesting statement, adds interest to your wall arrangement), if it's affordable, and if you don't hate it, go ahead and snap it up. You can always replace it when you find something you like better.

RULE #5: Work to create a pleasing ambience.

Your overall decorating goals should include creating an ambience that pleases all the senses.

Soothing sounds, intoxicating aromas, sumptuous textures—all these add immeasurably to the overall sense of a beautifully decorated home.

RULE #6: Put something alive in every room.

This is one of the best ways to enhance your home's ambience—real flowers, green plants, funky-looking cacti, or a spaniel curled up on the rug.

RULE #7: Try to stage a surprise.

An element of the unexpected will do wonders for your décor—an oversized picture, a shelf hung lower than usual, a red pillow in a green room, a teacup turned on its side.

RULE #8: Don't put out everything you own.

If one lovely pitcher is good, twenty aren't necessarily better. In other words, there's a fine line between cozy and cluttered. Even if you love that rich Victorian look with knickknacks everywhere, try to avoid the trap of too much of everything. You can always store away your extra treasures or rotate them seasonally.

Rules Made to Be Broken
(Decorating Assumptions You Can Ignore)

MYTH #1: "Don't use white—it shows dirt."

As long as they're washable and bleachable, pure white slipcovers, curtains, towels, and rugs can actually be the most practical accessories of all.

MYTH #2: "It all has to match."

In fact, a mix of styles, colors, and periods can be visually exciting. Just try to have a common element, such as a color or design motif, to tie them all together.

MYTH #3: "You need a round cloth for a round table."

Draped beautifully, or even tied up at the corners, a square or rectangular cloth will do just fine on any table.

MYTH #4: "You need a sofa, a chair, and a coffee table."

Try to get rid of your preconceived notions about what you "ought" to have in a room and think instead of what you need to happen in that room. You don't necessarily need a coffee table; you need something to unify the seating arrangement and to hold magazines and refreshments.

MYTH #5: "When in doubt, use beige; it goes with everything."

The grain of truth in this common assumption is that neutral colors can be very relaxing and usually blend easily with other colors. But beige is far from the only neutral! Any "earth color"—white, black, gray, brown, terra-cotta, and especially green and blue—can serve the same purpose and be far more interesting.

MYTH #6: "The sofa goes up against the wall."

Not always! Instead of lining up the furniture square against the wall, try setting some pieces at an angle or creating several small conversational groups away from the walls. You may end up making better, more interesting use of the space.

MYTH #7: "Paint small rooms pale colors to make them look bigger."

It's not necessarily bad to paint your tiny study pale yellow—but it may not be your best choice. Dark paint in a small room can emphasize its cozy character. Conversely, painting a large room a pale neutral can emphasize its airiness. Think of the statement you want to make, not what rules you've read.

MYTH #8: "Anything goes."

While encouraging you to break free from decorating "ought to's" and the demands of others, we do want to remind you that certain classical principles still prevail—principles of balance, harmony, and comfort. Experiment boldly. Break the rules. But at the same time ask yourself: Is this balanced? Will we be able to live with this? Do these things go together? Does this really work?

If the answer is yes, the result will be a truly beautiful home.

One More Rule:
Rule #9: Don't always follow the rules!

4

How to Think (or Rethink) a Room

Basic Principles for Putting Your Home Together

THERE YOU ARE, in the middle of your living room (or bedroom or bath or office), wondering what to do to make it look fabulous. Where do you start?

Whether you're staring at four empty walls or a roomful of furniture you can't afford to get rid of, you start at the same place—where you are, and with what you have. After that, here are a few guidelines to help you move forward.

PRINCIPLE #1: Build from the basics.

When you're rethinking a room, don't even think about accessories or wall decoration at first. Instead, start with the big picture—the basic furnishings that you have (or need) and their arrangement in the room. Once you have the big pieces in place, you can add or subtract other elements to complete the picture. Arrangement always comes before accessories.

If you're starting from scratch, consider spending the bulk of your budget on a few good pieces that establish the heart of a room. When Emilie was furnishing the large "great room" in her current home, she actually hired a decorator to help her acquire just the right oversized English chintz sofa and loveseat and a custom-matched area rug. Then she filled in the rest of the room on her own, using much-less-expensive pieces.

PRINCIPLE #2: Become a frequent visitor.

It helps to pretend you're a guest in the room you want to decorate—and be a guest that visits frequently. Each time, try to look at the room with fresh eyes, as if you've never seen it. Get a feel for what is working, what is pleasing, what draws the eye, what disturbs the harmony of the room. Watch out also for objects that impede the traffic flow, for items that tend to be misplaced because they have no satisfactory home. As you rethink the room, you may be able to take care of these practical concerns as well.

PRINCIPLE #3: Think function instead of furniture.

In other words, instead of assuming that you need a sofa, a chair, a coffee table, and a rug, consider that you need comfortable seating, a place for somebody to lie down, something to tie the furniture grouping together visually, and a place to put drinks and magazines. Looking at your needs this way will help you open your mind to more creative options—and it may remind you of needs you hadn't considered. You may realize, for instance, that you need places for two people to lie down, a comfortable spot for people who like to sit on the floor, and something that soothes your back after a long day. Instead of the sofa-chair-coffee-table combo, you may end up with two matching sofas, several small tables, a pile of floor pillows, and a therapeutic rocking chair.

PRINCIPLE #4: Fix your focus.

Probably the most important thing you need to decide for each room is where you want the focus; that is, what you want people to see first when they enter the room. A room's focal point is its anchor, its center of gravity, so you'll want to arrange the rest of the room to play up that focus. You'll find ideas for doing just that in chapter 5.

PRINCIPLE #5: Consider a room's "body language."

Many factors affect the arrangement of furniture in a room: lighting, comfort, visual balance, and utility. But one thing to remember as you arrange the major items is that a room can actually appear to "open its arms" to people or to "turn its back" on them. Try to keep this in mind as you consider where to place your furniture. Try to keep a clear visual line from the entryway to the major seating areas. Even chairs that are grouped around a fireplace can be angled so that they appear to invite visitors over.

PRINCIPLE #6: Use color to tie a room together.

Color decisions will depend on many factors—your preferences, the effect you want to create, colors of existing furnishings or carpet, current fashion, and so on. But always remember that color is one of the easiest—and least expensive—ways to make a statement and unify a room. A set of print pillows in the right colors can pull together your grandma's green chair, your husband's blue-matted print, and your pink-cushioned sofa.

A touch of black can be especially effective in adding an elegant note to almost any room. It doesn't have to be much—a lamp shade, a narrow picture frame, the background in a rug.

PRINCIPLE #7: Fill in with imaginative accessories.

This is where you can have fun and also save the most money. The rest of this book is filled with imaginative ideas for adding inexpensive sparkle to your walls, tables, and floors.

PRINCIPLE #8: Keep squinting.

Use the squint test during the rethinking process to test for balance of placement and silhouette. If you're not sure whether a floor plan or wall arrangement works, squint your eyes until everything goes a little fuzzy. The details won't distract you, and you'll be able to see the big picture more clearly.

PRINCIPLE #9: Don't go it alone.

For most people we know, decorating is more fun when you have someone to share opinions with as well as the work. This can be especially helpful when you feel stuck for new ideas. Invite a friend over to help you move furniture around, create wall arrangements, or sort through your junk for treasures. And don't forget to talk to your husband, your children, and anyone else who lives in the house. Their opinions count, too.

Bright Ideas

Ten Alternatives to a Coffee Table

✿ *An ottoman with a tray on top*

✿ *A row of wicker bed trays*

✿ *Three chairs (either "singles" or extra ones from the dining room)*

✿ *A stack of old suitcases (with travel stickers!) or wooden boxes*

✿ *Nothing! Just leave the center of the room bare.*

✿ *A tray on a base*

✿ *A child's wagon, wooden or metal, with pull handle wired in place*

✿ *A large round planter (wooden keg, clay pot, cement urn) with glass on top (If you want, put something interesting inside!)*

✿ *A collection of small individual tables*

✿ *A backless wooden garden bench*

5

Finding Your Focus

The Art of Anchoring a Room

WHERE DOES YOUR EYE FALL FIRST when you enter a wonderful, inviting room?

That item is the room's focal point, and it's one of your first considerations in decorating. The focal point is the room's anchor. It's the item that sets the general mood for the decor.

Finding your focus in decorating isn't as complicated as it sounds. It's simply a matter of being aware where the eye will go in a given room and then playing that natural movement up or down according to your purposes.

Most focal points result from a blend of room arrangement and practical necessity. In fact, many rooms come with a built-in focal point—the sofa, the dining table, the bed, or perhaps a fireplace or wonderful picture window. Other rooms can be deliberately arranged around a focal point that you select—a huge, eye-catching painting, for instance, or a cozy conversational center. Occasionally you will need to arrange a focus to distract the eye from a natural but undesirable focal point—an ugly fireplace, or perhaps a television that you don't want to dominate the room.

How do you determine a room's focal point? The easiest way is usually to arrange the furniture in a way that seems comfortable, then make a lot of little trips in and out of the room, cruising through it, coming back through the entry, trying to get a feel for what stands out.

Does your eye always return to the big picture window and the lovely shade trees in the front yard? That view is your natural focus. All you need to do to make that room wonderful is to keep the window treatments simple, the glass sparkling, and the furniture arranged so everyone can enjoy the outdoors.

Do you have an item you absolutely love—an art print, a family heirloom, a beloved collection? That can be your focal point, too. Give your special item a place of honor and arrange the rest of the room to call attention to it.

Does the big antique armoire that wouldn't fit anywhere else immediately draw your attention? Why not let the armoire be the room's focal point? Leave the doors open (or even reverse the doors so that any decorative carving shows when the doors are open) and fill the piece to overflowing with interesting items—a stack of antique linens, a basket of yarn, a box of old toys.

In rooms such as bedrooms and dining rooms, the focal point will almost inevitably be tied to the purpose of the room—the bed, decked out in a colorful quilt, or the dining table, festively set or uncovered and gleaming. And any oversized or unusual piece will attempt to be the focal point of the room where it lives. In many cases it makes sense to accept that reality.

If you are unable to settle on a focal point in a given room, or if for some reason the natural focus is undesirable, use your imagination to create a new focal point. Rearrange the furniture to play up another part of the room. Or arrange several small pieces together into an interesting vignette that draws the eye.

Try an arrangement of primitive musical instruments on a wall next to a painted Mexican chair from an import store. Or flank a small bureau with two chairs and top with an antique scale filled with lemons. Hang a big gilt mirror or a couple of botanical prints on the wall over it. Don't be shy. Have fun clustering interesting items to stage a statement!

Keep in mind that a large room or a series of rooms that flow together in an "open" design could easily have a number of focal points—areas that catch the eye and move it along. In Emilie's "great room," for instance, the eye moves from the big fireplace with its "barn" painting to the floral-chintz oversized sofas to the armoire full of china teacups to the collection of black-and-white family photos.

Even Yoli's tiny beach-cottage living room has more than one focus—the sofa with its bevy of pillows and the big painted tray hanging behind it, the stone fireplace with its simple iron sconce, and the carefully crafted vignette of a painted bureau, two French chairs, an antique mirror with silk festoon, and an arrangement of china plates and botanical prints.

Here are some more ideas for fixing the focus in your rooms.

Sofa Savvy

Making your sofa a focal point is a simple, natural tactic, and it places a subtle emphasis on comfort and conversation. Upholstered in a lovely pattern (or slip-covered with a great fabric), adorned with puffy pillows in a variety of shapes and colors, and backed with an eye-catching wall decoration, the sofa easily anchors a room.

Wonderful Windows

If you have a beautiful view, all you really need is a dramatically simple window treatment—perhaps just a set of sheer curtains drawn to the side or a shaped valance to frame the view—or nothing at all. Even with an unattractive view, a window can make an effective focal point if you make it part of an interesting vignette. Hide the view with sheer fabric stretched on tension rods, place an interesting chair nearby to catch the light, add a potted tree and a wall arrangement.

Mirror Magic

Mirrors make a beautifully dramatic focus for any room, especially as part of an arranged vignette. An old, thrift-store mirror with a beat-up frame can look wonderful arranged over a little commode or bench that holds a potted plant or a bowl of potpourri. Or combine a mirror with a glass shelf resting on architectural corbels and holding a vase or small sculpture that looks pretty reflected in the mirror. A number of small framed mirrors together increases the reflective possibilities.

Fireplace Focus

Fireplaces are another one of those inevitable focal points that don't need a lot of extra decoration. A simple large mirror or painting, a few candlesticks, or perhaps a group of metal sconces are all you really need. Cut down on clutter by grouping your fireplace implements in a vase or umbrella stand or hanging them on a rack.

If the fireplace is not functional or is out of business for the season, you can cover the hearth with interesting architectural pieces such as an old iron gate or a little picket fence. Or fill the hearth area with green plants, an arrangement of topiaries, a group of little chairs, a large painting—use your imagination.

If you don't have a real fireplace, a faux fireplace makes a wonderfully warm focal point for a room. Simply install an old mantel from a building supply company or an antique shop. Cover the hearth area with a screen or other decor and decorate as if the fireplace were real.

Dining Drama

Whether in a formal dining room or a corner of the kitchen or den, a dining table and chairs provide a natural and essential focal point. If the dining set is beautiful in itself, leave it uncovered and bare—or play up its beauty with a simple bowl of fruit or vase of fresh flowers. If the furniture is less than wonderful, the creative use of table coverings, slipcovers, and centerpieces can still draw the eye. A chandelier or light fixture should shed light on the table rather than calling attention to itself.

The Big "Thing"

Occasionally a room will contain an object that commands attention just because of its size. Grandma's carved sideboard, Aunt Edith's piano, the mirrored armoire you love but don't really have room for—if you have an item like this, you can either make it a focal point or diminish its importance by focusing attention elsewhere.

If the piano reflects your love of music, why not emphasize this musical aspect of the room? Frame an old piece of sheet music and hang it on the wall—or decorate the wall with old banjos, violins, drums, or tambourines. Paint an old magazine rack or decoupage it with sheet music; tuck it beside the piano bench to hold music. Cover the bench with a wonderful fabric and choose an interesting lamp.

The Magic Eye

It's almost too easy to let the television be the focus of a living room or den. With a little ingenuity you can keep the TV accessible without letting it be the center of attention. Try tucking it into an armoire with doors or shutters. Or place it high or low, out of

The best houses seem to "come from the heart," and are created by people who know who they are and express it.

—Charlotte Moss

the general field of vision. In Emilie's great room, the large TV is tucked low to the side of the room. In Yoli's living room, the small TV rests high on a column behind the main furniture group—and you don't notice it unless you look.

Bright Ideas
No Nails!

If you don't want to put nail holes in your stone fireplace, hang decorations from the ceiling. Simply install a small hook in the ceiling and use thin wire, plastic fishing line, or even silk cording to hang your wreath, picture, or mirror. Large items can also simply be leaned on the mantel.

This method is easily adapted to walls as well. Borrow a tip from your great-grandmother and hang pictures from a cord attached at ceiling level. One of Yoli's favorite wall decorations is a painted wooden tray hung from the ceiling with gold silk cord tassels.

6

The Quest for Decorating Magic

Treasure Hunting Outside Your Home

SOMETHING OLD, SOMETHING NEW, something borrowed . . . it's not just a wedding formula, it's also the secret to decorating beautifully on a budget.

You start with loving and using what you have, of course, but sooner or later you probably will need to shop. (Besides, that's half the fun.) And the secret to shopping without blowing your budget is learning to find decorating gold in the least-likely places.

To maintain a rich look on a not-so-rich budget, however, we suggest shopping with the 25-75 rule in mind. That is, the bulk of your decor can come from very inexpensive sources and even be of poor quality—but your "cheap chic" treasures should be balanced with a few pieces of real, lasting quality. At least

25 percent of your furnishings and accessories should feature quality materials and workmanship—a beautiful oak chair, a fine-art print, or a lovely bed to balance your discount-store linens, junk-shop mirror, and import-store blinds. Also, be sure to visit quality stores or antique shops on a regular basis to keep your eye trained toward quality.

Where do we go to find decorating bargains? Following are some of our favorite sources.

A Circle of Friends

The best bargains are those that cost nothing at all—and that's what you may find in your mother's attic, your neighbor's garage, your sister's back porch. Family, friends, and neighbors can all be great resources. If you see something you think you can use, it never hurts to ask if you can have it, buy it, or swap for it. Sometimes it's even possible to arrange a long-term loan.

The reverse also applies, of course. If you have some pieces that just don't fit where you live now, why not offer them to the newlyweds down the street?

The Flea Factor

Garage sales, swap meets, flea markets, and estate sales are classic and dependable sources of decorating bargains. The value of these sources, however, may depend on where you live. In some areas, for instance, flea markets are merely large-scale antique dealerships with inflated prices for poor merchandise. In other places they are sources of pure decorating gold. Garage sales and swap meets flourish in certain areas and offer practically nothing elsewhere. Estate sales, auctions, or church rummage sales may provide better bargains in large cities than in small towns. It shouldn't take more than a few weekends of treasure hunting to locate the best sources for your area.

Accumulating Goodwill

Goodwill Industries, the Salvation Army, and an array of other charity organizations offer inexpensive items for sale as well as supplying jobs for those in need. The selection will change every day and the best items will disappear quickly, so visit often. It helps to make friends with the staff and ask to be called if certain items come in. Be aware, however, that many of these organizations now recognize the value of "collectibles." Don't assume that an item is a bargain unless you've compared it with similar items elsewhere.

In addition, ask if you can look through the back lot or the discard pile. An item that has not been deemed reparable may give you the raw materials you need for decorating magic. Look for interesting parts of worn or broken furniture, for rusted tools with interesting shapes, for broken jewelry that could be used to decorate another item.

"Junque" Shops and Antique Malls

These can be wonderful resources if you know what you want and understand what you see. Not

everything you see in an antique store is an antique—
you'll see reproductions and ten-year-old items among
the truly old pieces. And not everything in these shops
is a bargain—the owners are usually savvy to trends
and quick to ask what the market can command. But
these stores can be great sources of unique accessories if you know what you like and you stick to your
budget. Look for not-quite-perfect pieces (a chipped
plate, a cracked vase). And remember that the older
furniture in these places, even if not a "steal," may still
be far sturdier and less expensive than a comparable
new piece.

The "Marts"

These are the large discount stores where you go
to buy your paper towels, your school supplies, and
almost everything else. They also frequently offer
attractive but inexpensive linens, knickknacks,
posters, and even furniture. The biggest drawback to
these items is that everyone else in America shops at
these stores and may recognize the discount-store
treasures—you'll need to muster some creativity to
keep your house from shouting, "Attention, shoppers!"
Keep an eye on what you like and then shop the sales
for the very best bargains.

Closing Out

Three kinds of closeout stores offer great bargain
shopping for the home.

First, there are outlet stores, which often congre-
gate in specialized outlet malls. These typically offer

manufacturing "seconds" as well as merchandise from previous seasons. If you have an outlet mall nearby, you may be able to go to town on buying linens, dishes, even silk flowers. Do a little retail window-shopping first, though, to make sure your bargains are truly bargains. Second, there are stores that specialize in "aged" merchandise, primarily clothing. Many of these stock designer brands from previous seasons, and most of them offer home items as well. Look for sheets, towels, wastebaskets, kitchen supplies, even books.

In addition to these more upscale outlets are the "super bargain" stores—sort of large scale five-and-dimes. The quality may range from very good to simply awful, but the prices are usually rock bottom. Look for paper goods, craft supplies, candles, inexpensive dishes, curtain rods. But remember . . . not knowing what you will find is half the fun.

"Make It Yourself" Shopping

Increasingly the craft-store chains are one-stop shopping resources for almost any kind of decorating. This is the place to buy silk and dried flowers, paint and paintbrushes, and even unfinished wooden furniture. They also offer instruction books or even classes to help you brush up on your skills. Fabric stores, too, offer a wide variety of craft supplies as well as wonderful material and notions. Look for no-sew window treatments and lamp-shade supplies.

Hardware, Home, and Garden

In many areas, your neighborhood hardware store has grown into a one-stop center offering everything from garden supplies to paint. Let your imagination run wild as you wander the industrial-style aisles. These stores *are* especially good sources of lighting, garden items (planters, lawn furniture), and decorative details such as molding and knobs. In addition, they typically offer a wide variety of how-to books, and many offer weekend workshops as well.

In addition, large garden centers will offer a lot more than houseplants. Garden centers feature the widest variety of planters for use as vegetable bins, candleholders, towel holders and, well, planters. In addition you'll probably find birdhouses, birdbaths, wind chimes, interesting tools, garden furniture, and even small fountains, any of which could be used in your decorating scheme.

Despite the usefulness of the large home and garden chains, don't overlook your small mom-and-pop hardware store as a decorating resource. These are often the places to find unusual or quirky items the big chains neglect.

Import Interest

For interesting baskets, unusual furniture, inexpensive table settings, and all manner of inexpensive decorations, try your local import store. Useful finds include roll-up matchstick blinds, brightly painted plates and bowls, pillows and cushions in a wide range of colors, posters, imaginative candles, and wall decorations. The trick is to watch for true bargains and use your booty in such a way that your room doesn't look like a college dorm.

A Piece of a House

Larger cities often offer shops exclusively dedicated to selling parts of buildings—doors, windows, mantels, dresser crowns, "gingerbread," outdoor shutters. Seek these out for inspiration as well as for supplies. Then try to find similar items on your own. If you see a building being remodeled or torn down, it never hurts to ask. Or ask an antique or junk dealer if you can look at broken pieces—you might be able to rescue a wonderful bit of carving that transforms one of your walls.

Let Your Fingers Walk

Once you get on the mailing list for one catalog, many others will follow—or you can call to ask for a specific catalog. The best of these can save you time and money while offering access to sources you could never visit. For the best bargains, use the upscale catalogs to spot new trends and ideas, then order similar items from less-expensive catalogs.

Call in a Pro

Professional designers and store detailers have to go somewhere to get their stuff. For instance, in the Southern California area where we live, professionals go to a big swap meet once a month. If you have a designer friend who has access to these places, ask her to look for a certain item you need. Or consider paying a professional to procure a certain item for you.

Bright Ideas

A Shopping Tip

If you are shopping garage sales or flea markets, plan to arrive either very early or very late. Early in the day, you'll find the best selection. Late in the day, you'll likely get the best prices—but the merchandise may be very picked over. If you attend an estate sale held in a home, consider that the furnishings in the main room of the house may be high priced and quickly picked over. For the real bargains, head for the basement or attic for the overlooked "fixer uppers."

Love Is a Choice

Yoli's Decorating Story

AS A WOMAN STARTING OUT my design career, I had yet to develop my own sense of aesthetics or style. I loved everything that was beautiful, and every new client caused me to fall in love with a new look. I loved contemporary one day, Italian the next, was crazy for French, and oh, that adorable cluttered country look!

You can imagine what a mishmash my own house was beginning to be! It was fragmented and gave the word "eclectic" a new meaning. Although I loved designing for my clients, decorating for my own home was nothing but one big frustration. Every new fabric sample and "hot off the showroom shelf" accessory increased my discontent—and it didn't help to know that my own decorating budget was often much smaller than my clients'. When guests would come over, instead of welcoming them graciously, I would bore them with recitations about what I wanted to do in the house "someday."

I knew I couldn't go on this way. Thinking about what I didn't have was making me and my family miserable. So I started on a quest to find my own unique look and to love it because it was mine. Refusing to be tempted by every new style that came along, I chose instead to be grateful for what I did have and to look for its decorating potential. The beginning of my "love what you have" style was born.

Once I began looking at my home with that attitude, I discovered all sorts of wonderful treasures hidden around my home and in my mother's and grandmother's cupboards—beautiful old china, hoards of embroidered hankies, even a pair of interesting old eyeglasses. I also realized what a treasure trove of fabrics I had acquired over the years.

Fabric, you see, is one of my true joys. My heart starts beating faster when I enter a fabric store, and I can't resist a remnant table. My cabinets and storage boxes were simply bursting with a wonderful variety of material and trims. So it just seemed natural to make an exuberant mix of fabrics the basis for my unmatched style.

This decision, in turn, left me free to combine many styles in furniture and accessories—from gleaming antiques to garage-sale finds. I decided anything goes as long as it's beautiful, tasteful, and, of course, cozy and comfortable—something my family could enjoy.

My decision to love what I have and decorate on that basis was an important step in my personal decorating adventure. We're all unique, made up of different backgrounds, ethnic histories, and lifestyles. And we're all much more interesting than we think we are. So start expressing your uniqueness in your home and decide to love what you have.

7

A Creative Decorator's Toolbox

♥

What You Need to Make Your Decorating Life Easier

IF YOU'RE ALREADY an accomplished seamstress and an experienced carpenter, you're probably already well equipped to create a beautiful home on a budget. But if you're just starting out, you might appreciate a list of the basics. These are tools we find we use almost every day in decorating—some obvious choices and some surprises.

Keep your decorating tools handy in an easy-to-grab caddy or toolbox. Craft stores and hardware stores feature wonderful possibilities—we especially like the kind that doubles as a stepstool. But even a big basket or a cardboard box wrapped in pretty paper will serve in a pinch.

Sticky Stuff

For attaching almost anything to anything, keep a glue gun on hand. A small one will be adequate for most jobs. Use it to glue ribbons to the edge of a lamp shade, attach shells to a chair rail, or stick silk flowers onto a hat. For attaching paper or fabric to larger surfaces, however, you might find that spray adhesive works better.

A Tacky Subject

A staple gun is an invaluable tool for small upholstery jobs or large wall coverings. You can even use your staple gun to shirr fabric over a window for a curtain. Thumbtacks and pushpins are useful for attaching fabrics to wood and holding items in place while you are stapling. They can also be great for hanging lightweight objects—such as a small picture on a ribbon.

Elastic Hold

You'd be surprised what you can do with a rubber band! Use it to make poufs and roses in fabric—just tighten the band around a loop of fabric and fluff fabric to hide the band. Cover a wastebasket by wrapping fabric around it and securing with a rubber band, or secure scarves around a pillow form by banding the four corners. Keep in mind, though, that the rubber will deteriorate in a couple of years and need to be replaced. If you prefer, use plastic twist ties that come on a roll.

Hanging Hardware

You never know when you might need a nail or a screw, so keep a small assortment of each handy. Also useful are plastic anchors to use with drywall, cup hooks and bulldog hangers, and screw eyes and picture wire.

Toolbox Basics

If you have nails or hangers, you need a hammer—preferably the clawed kind. If you have screws, you must have a screwdriver. You need at least one slot-type screwdriver and a Phillips variety. It helps to have a small variety of sizes. Less basic but still handy are C-clamps for securing glued items and a level.

Cutting Remarks

For cutting fabrics, a good pair of scissors is a must, but the inexpensive plastic-handled kind work beautifully. Another pair of utility scissors may also be helpful, as well as one of those utility knives with the triangular blades. If you find that you like to do a lot of architectural decorating—working with lattice, molding and the like—you might consider investing in a good handsaw or lightweight saber saw. You'll find, however, that most hardware stores are happy to cut materials to your measurements.

Taking Your Measure

At very least, you need a good yardstick and a retractable metal tape measure. A T-square can also be helpful, especially if you're the personality type that likes things *really* straight.

Material Assets

If you can use one, a sewing machine will pay infinite dividends. But even without a machine, you can still work a lot of fabric magic. You will need a steam/dry iron and an ironing board or a table you can pad with blankets or towels. An assortment of pins (straight and safety, plus heavyweight "T" pins for slipcovers) is invaluable, plus a packet of large needles and heavyweight thread. Fusible interfacings and fabric glue will enable you to "sew" without sewing. Even shirring tape, pleating tape, and window-shades kits—all invaluable time-savers—are available in iron-on form.

Touch-Up Tools

Our friend Donna lists spray paint as her single most valuable decorating tool. She even spray-painted her kitchen cabinets once. And while we wouldn't necessarily recommend that, we do believe that paint is one of the simplest and most versatile ways to decorate. We recommend that you keep on hand an assortment of painting supplies: several sizes of good-quality brushes, masking tape, a packet of sandpaper.

One of Yoli's favorite all-purpose decorating tools is a gold-paint pen from the hobby store. She uses hers almost constantly to touch up a chandelier, to add a spark to a silk arrangement, to decorate candles and candlesticks—anywhere a little touch of gold is needed. For small areas, the pen is much handier than gold paint and a brush. You can even "vein" a lamp base—especially effective on black.

A Leg to Stand On

Unless you are extremely tall, you'll need a tall stepstool, a small ladder, or a tall friend to help you paint or hang items above your head.

Your Ingenuity

Sooner or later, you'll encounter a situation where you just don't have the standard tool to do the job. When that happens, put the right tool on your "to buy" list, and then look around for something that might work just as well. If you can't find a pin, try glue. If you don't have a tape measure, use a yardstick. Or go next door and borrow the tools you need from a neighbor (bake her some cookies later as a thank-you).

As long as you keep safety in mind (don't substitute a rickety chair for a ladder), whatever works is an appropriate tool!

8

Fabulous Fabrics

Making the Most of Your Material Assets

WHETHER NEW OR VINTAGE, draped, pleated, or shirred, fabric is one of your most important decorating tools. And you don't need to be a seamstress to make beautiful use of fabrics in your home.

Instead of sewing, you can staple, fuse, glue, tie, or simply drape a variety of fabrics into window coverings, pillows, slipcovers, or even room dividers. Fabrics lend warmth and texture to your decorating scheme, they are easily cleaned and freshened, and they can be changed even more quickly for simple, inexpensive redecorating.

Slipcovers, for example, are a recently rediscovered magic wand. A simple change of slipcovers can transform a room in an instant. Clean white cotton covers give you a cool summer background for a set of pillows in bright primary colors—or ice-cream pastels, or another set in brown-and-gold basket tones. As the weather cools, darker slipcovers in rich colors and sumptuous textures—flannel, velvet, corduroy, or even chenille—invite the family to gather by the fire. What could be more festive than a set of holiday slipcovers in red-and-green plaid or a sunny yellow to welcome the spring?

A slipcover can be a carefully cut and fitted second skin for your sofa or chair. Or it can be as simple as a sheet or bedspread draped over a chair or sofa and pinned to fit. A set of fitted covers is certainly worth the investment of time or money, but don't be afraid to throw, drape, pin, and tie. (Use a wooden spatula to tuck the cover deep in the crevices of your furniture, and secure in hidden places with sturdy metal "T" pins.) If you have a futon, your slipcover options are especially easy—all you need is a fitted sheet slipped over the futon mattress and secured with pins in a hidden spot.

And remember that slipcovers are not just for sofas and easy chairs. It's easy to make covers to fit over folding chairs or simple dining room chairs—buy a simple commercial pattern, cut your own out of newspaper (the fit doesn't have to be perfect!), or again, simply drape or tie. A simple straight chair swathed in tulle and tied with a satin ribbon adds an instant romantic touch to a bedroom or a wedding reception. And a folding or straight chair can be instantly transformed by slipping a pillowcase over the back and tying the base with ribbon!

Fabric can cover and revitalize anything from a cardboard box to an antique lamp. Fabric covers are wonderful disguises for scarred or outdated furniture. An old leather-covered pedestal table puts on a romantic face when white brocade is draped over, tied underneath with a ribbon, and then poufed into graceful puddles on the floor. A glass top and a few matching pillows in the room are all that are needed to complete the picture.

An inexpensive round particle-board table from a discount store just needs a pretty fabric skirt to fit in stylishly with its surroundings. But instead of the familiar flounced table skirts, try covering it with a 1950s bridge cloth from a flea market. Or cover the top of the table with one piece of fabric and use your staple gun to shirr another length of fabric tightly around the edge. Glue ribbon around the edge to hide the staples.

Your staple gun, in fact, is a superb fabric companion. Use it to cover a footstool, attach fabric to the wall, or even to hang curtain panels. For a sumptuous look, pad the walls of a small alcove or nook with batting and then staple fabric over the batting. Secure at the ceiling level with strips of wooden molding or wide ribbon glued to cover the staples.

The possibilities for fabric as a wall covering are endless. Pleat the fabric neatly on the wall. Stretch it tightly. Or buy an entire bolt of fabric that is languishing on the sale table because of a dye-lot problem that makes it unsuitable for clothing. Shirred tightly on a wall and secured with staples, this same fabric reject will give a room a soft, romantic flavor, and the imperfections will be hidden by the shirring.

Fabric also has wonderful possibilities for doors and screens. Ready-to-finish hinged screens are easy to find in catalogs and craft stores, but you can make your own by covering plywood panels with fabric and using piano hinges to hold the panels together. Or even more simply, hang a simple fabric panel from a curtain rod.

Yoli did this in her own bedroom to replace a set of ugly folding closet doors. Her daughter, Joy, gave her the idea of removing the doors altogether and curtaining off the closet space. So Yoli's clothes now nestle behind a set of festive black-and-white polka-dot curtains with black velvet ribbon tabs.

Don't overlook fabric as a decoration in itself. Stretched on a frame like a painter's canvas (these frames are easily available in art supply stores) and either framed or left unframed, a boldly designed fabric can take the place of a painting or print. Hung from a quilt frame or simply stapled to a strip of wood, an inexpensive afghan or throw becomes a wall tapestry. Upholstery remnants can be framed as pictures or used to cover picture mats. Swaths of fabric can be used very effectively to drape mirrors and picture frames—just staple or tack in place behind the frame and catch at the side with ribbon or silk cord. With such a curtain, a mirror can even masquerade as another window!

The two most obvious uses for fabrics in the home, of course, are as pillows and window coverings. And now is the best time ever for using fabrics creatively to make fabulous and easy cushions and curtains—even without sewing a seam.

A famous designer once proclaimed that one can never have too many pillows. We think he's right. Pillows not only lend an air of comfort to a home, they also provide a quick, easy, and inexpensive way to set a mood or tie together mismatched pieces with color.

If you have even rudimentary skills with a sewing machine, of course, your pillow possibilities are endless. It's easy to sew two fabric squares or rectangles together, turn them inside out, and stuff with fiberfill or a foam pillow form. It's only a little bit more complicated to add zippers or Velcro so the covers can be washed, to make the shapes more complex, and to add piping, cord, ruffles, or other decorations. (Check your fabric or craft store for easy directions.) Make use of fabric remnants by crafting small scatter pillows (try tucking in a little pouch of herbs or potpourri for a wonderful fragrance) or sewing together in a simple patchwork. Or rescue the embroidery from a worn pillowcase by cutting it out and appliqueing onto another pillow. You can even make a collection of pillow covers (perhaps with seasonal themes) that attach to a basic pillow with buttons.

Don't sew—or don't have the time? Cover your old pillows (or even a pillow form) with scarves or dish towels knotted at the corners, tacked around the edges, or tied like packages. Use fabric glue to attach buttons, bows, tassels, appliques, or almost any decoration to the top of a plain pillow from the discount store. For a different look, try tucking a standard-size bed pillow into a king-sized pillowcase and tying the extra fabric at one end (or both ends) with silk cord or ribbon. You'll have a pretty pillow "pouch" with flowing fabric at the ends—almost like a gift-wrapped package.

Sew-free window coverings are just as easy and very much in style these days. We've found so many wonderful possibilities, in fact, that we've devoted an entire chapter to creating wonderful windows!

Fabulous fabrics for home decorating don't have to come from the local fabric store—although it's fun to play amid all the myriad patterns and colors. If you keep your eyes open, you'll begin to see fabric possibilities everywhere you look.

Sheets, for instance, belong in the decorator's hall of fame for their many uses. These decorating wonders not only come in a variety of colors and patterns but offer ample yardage—no need to sew lengths of fabric together. They are often available for a pittance in closeout or discount stores, and white sales offer an opportunity to snap them up at bargain prices. Packaged sheet sets offer a ready-made mix of patterns and colors for table coverings, pillows, and curtains. (When buying sheets, however, do compare prices with yardages from fabric stores. Unless you shop carefully, you might not be getting a bargain.)

What can you do with a sheet? Cut to size and hemmed—or simply draped—a sheet makes a lovely tablecloth—and a matching set of napkins is easily crafted from the extra yardage or from matching pillowcases. (If you don't sew, hem with fusible tape, or just use the sheet as it is.) Drape the "tablecloth" so that the pretty printed hem shows; very few guests will walk around the table to see if you have the same edge on the other side.

A flat sheet with a broad hem quickly becomes an instant curtain; just thread a curtain rod through the hem—or sew a simple seam a couple of inches from the top to create a ruffled, country-looking "header."

The wide yardage of sheets makes them natural wall coverings. And sheets make great slipcovers. To dress a wicker chair for the winter, simply drape a dark flannel sheet over it, tie the sheet in back, and anchor it with a coordinating chair cushion.

Bedspreads picked up at import stores, garage sales, or even your own attic can masquerade as slipcovers, room dividers, or window coverings. Terrycloth hand towels on tension rods make adorable (and washable) curtains for small kitchen or bathroom windows. Discarded drapes in rich fabrics can be cleaned and used for a number of purposes—room dividers, table coverings, even clever pillows cut to show off the pleated headings.

And vintage linens—tea towels, hankies, doilies, lace tablecloths—are beautiful whether they are tacked onto pillows, cut into curtains, draped over valance poles, tucked into vases, or just allowed to be their own sweet selves. Old hankies, available for a few dollars at the most from antique stores (or your grandma's bureau), make lovely, romantic napkins to use with your finest china tea service. Monogrammed napkins or towels can become lamp shades, pillows, or sachet covers.

Even discarded clothing can provide you with raw material for fabric-rich decorating. Worn-out jeans can reappear as novelty pillows, rag rugs, or even place mats (keep the pockets, and tuck in a bandanna to use as a napkin). Those adorable, hand-crafted children's clothes can become soft-sculpture pillows (just sew the openings closed and stuff), wall decorations (frame in a shadow box or just hang from a peg), new outfits for dolls or stuffed animals. Shawls and scarves can be beautifully draped around mirrors, bedposts, or the backs of chairs. Years ago, Yoli's yellow-and-white checked maternity dress reappeared as billowy curtains for the baby's room!

Concerned about combining fabrics and matching colors? If you're really insecure, you can buy already matched patterns, but it's really rather difficult to go wrong. You can successfully mix as many as ten patterns if you keep a common color as a thread. Combine stripes, small prints and large, geometrics and plaids, jacquards, damask, novelty prints—you name it—but tie them all together with a common color.

Alternately, for a very small space or a room filled with mismatched furniture, try using one fabric throughout—for slipcovers, pillow, window coverings. The look can be quite sophisticated, and you may well be able to arrange a discount by ordering the fabric in bulk.

One of the big advantages of decorating with fabrics is that much of it is washable or easily cleaned. If you plan to pop your fabric creations into the washer, it's a good idea to prewash them before sewing or tacking to allow for shrinkage. If you're using older fabrics, of course, you will want to wash or clean them before using. Otherwise, use fabrics straight from the store with the "sizing" intact; this treatment will help the fabric resist stains and fading. Then, when your pillows or slipcovers or wall coverings or other fabulous fabric creations start looking a bit worn—just replace them. It'll be just as easy and fun the second time around!

Bright Ideas

*20 Things You Can Do with
Two Yards of Fabric*

Whenever you see a length of cute, cheap fabric on a sale table, snap it up! You'll be surprised at all the uses you'll find for it.

- ❀ *Pad and cover a dime-store footstool.*

- ❀ *Recover the seats in four metal folding chairs.*

- ❀ *Tuck behind a window treatment as an accent.*

- ❀ *Hem, add ribbons, and tie onto a simple rod for a bathroom-window valance.*

- ❀ *Drape over a small side table or nightstand.*

- ❀ *Use a kit to make a small lamp shade.*

- ❀ *Pink or hem edges and tie around a contrasting pillow.*

- ❀ *Cut into four pieces and sew to create two big pillows.*

- ❀ *Gather onto grosgrain ribbon and add a contrasting pocket to make an apron.*

- ❀ *Cut into fourths, hem, and use as napkins. Or cut smaller and use as cocktail napkins or coasters.*

- ✿ Pink or fringe edges and use to line drawers or baskets.

- ✿ "Paper" the interior of a cabinet.

- ✿ Gather around a small wastebasket or flowerpot; hold in place with rubber bands.

- ✿ Cover a photo mat or picture frame.

- ✿ Stretch like a canvas or frame like a picture.

- ✿ Wrap a present (use glue gun and fabric ribbon).

- ✿ Make a dirty-clothes bag for your child's room.

- ✿ Disguise an ugly lamp. Set lamp on large circle of fabric and bring up fabric like a pouch, tie just under shade with ribbon, raffia, or a covered rubber band.

- ✿ Cover a cardboard box for pretty storage (attach with spray adhesive).

- ✿ Tear into strips and crochet into a small bowl, basket, or rug.

9

Making Light

Candles, Lamps, and Other Bright Ideas

"LET THERE BE LIGHT!"

It was the Creator's first concern when starting construction on our beautiful home planet. And it's *one* of the most important ingredients in making any home beautiful and comfortable.

If you've ever smiled at someone you love across a warmly lit room, stretched out like a cat on a sunlit porch ... or squinted to read in a dimly lit bedroom, you know how important light can be. The way a home is lit will affect both its comfort and its ambience.

And actual light isn't the only decorating consideration when it comes to lighting. The sources of light—lamps, chandeliers, candles, "cans," and window treatments—are also part of the decor, just as important to visual effect as chairs and paintings.

Fortunately, light and lighting provide one of the easiest and most effective ways for you to decorate beautifully on a budget.

What kind of lighting do you need in your home?

First of all, you'll need general or ambient lighting to allow you to see. In the daytime, this may consist primarily of natural light from windows or skylights. In darker houses, and in the evening, some sort of artificial lighting—lamps, chandeliers, even candles—is needed. Because the light from overhead fixtures tends to be harsh, we prefer to rely mostly on lamps and other sources to supply most of our ambient light.

Task lighting provides the brighter, more focused light people need for specific purposes—reading, sewing, craft work, playing the piano. Many specialized fixtures are available for this purpose, from three-way lamps that supply more wattage when you need it to gooseneck lamps for the office, shaded task lights for the piano, and special lamps for bedtime reading. In general, work rooms such as kitchens, offices, and sewing rooms will need both more general lighting and more task lighting.

The third kind of lighting to consider in your home is the kind that affects the mood, sets the ambience, and provides visual accents throughout the house. Candlelight (or firelight) is a wonderful example of this kind of decorative lighting, but incandescent lights with warm-colored bulbs and gently diffusing shades can provide a similar effect. We like to use accent/ambience lighting in abundance around a home—on the bathroom counter, in a high cabinet or bookshelf, even in a window. Miniature lamps, groupings of candlesticks, wall-mounted sconces, even a candle next to the kitchen sink provide warm touches as well as adding surprisingly to the overall ambient light.

Where do you put a light? The arrangement of light sources in a room does make a difference. You need at least one light source in each corner of a room to define the perimeter. Big, eye-catching lamps should balance small ones. Brighter task lights should be situated where they can be used—next to chairs or beds. Careful use of shades (both window and lamp) should prevent glare. And consider the shadows in a room as well as the light sources—certain lamps may throw strange, unwanted patterns on the wall.

The amount and kinds of light in a room may even influence the way you decorate that room. A garden room or screened porch with lots of sunshine might be wonderful for plants but less appropriate for fine art or fadeable fabrics. A shaded, cozy room might be more appropriate for sleeping or snuggling than for studying or crafts.

Any room, however, is an appropriate home for beautiful, eye-catching, and affordable lamps.

Good-looking lamps are easy to find even in discount stores or home centers, and striking older lamps may be found at garage sales and flea markets. But you don't have to settle for what you can find in stores and shops. Today more than ever, it's easy to create your own custom lamps and shades.

Hobby and hardware stores offer the necessary equipment to turn almost any object into a lamp base, and old lamps from junk stores, antique stores, or your neighbor's garage can easily be rewired or remodeled.

Fabric and craft stores offer easy kits and instructions for covering lamp shades in a variety of fabrics—or you can buy a ready-made lamp shade and decorate or recover it on your own.

One of the favorite attractions in Yoli's kitchen is the little lamp she made from a blue spackleware coffeepot, available for almost nothing from a five-and-dime. Not only was it inexpensive, it adds a lively touch of warmth, humor, and old-fashioned fun to the room. With a little creativity, you can put together your own clever lamp—or have it done for you at a local lamp or electric shop. If you're ambitious, you can even create a floor lamp from a carved pole, a wooden base, a lamp harp from the hardware store, and a shade kit.

Chandeliers and hanging fixtures are other sources of decorative light. These range in style from elaborate crystal fountains to simple bulbs under enamel shades. The more elaborate fixtures can be quite expensive, but if you keep your eyes open you may find a real bargain at a remodeling sale. For a great "retro" look, use a wire brush to scrape the paint off an old fixture and retouch with gold paint. For a less formal effect, take advantage of rice-paper shades and hanging lamp kits from an import store. You can even remove the handle of an old wok lid, paint the lid with enamel paint, and transform it into a hanging lamp shade.

What about "cans" and track lighting?

These should be used carefully to avoid an unflattering effect, but they can be effective in outlining the perimeter of rooms or spotlighting a focal point such as a painting or vignette. In general, this kind of lighting suits a simpler, more contemporary decor.

You can make a can light or spotlight serve a very romantic purpose, however, by filtering it through a sheer drape. Try hanging a sheer curtain from a wrought-iron rod in front of a corner spotlight. Place a little vignette in front of the drape—a chair, a trunk, a little basket, and the overall effect will be quite charming.

Whatever the kind of lamp or fixture you buy, pick bulbs that give the warmest, most pleasing effect. In general this will mean incandescent bulbs, especially the pink-tinted kind. "Warm" fluorescents may provide a pleasing effect for less cost, and plants seem to thrive on fluorescent light. A rheostat or dimmer connected to an outlet or even an overhead fixture will make it easy to adjust the light for various needs. And for an instant rosy glow in any room, try the old trick of draping a pink scarf or hankie over a lamp.

Electric lights, of course, are not your only possible source of beautiful lighting. Candles and oil lamps also provide soft, flattering light. Emilie especially loves the miniature crystal oil lamps that can be purchased through mail order or in gift shops; she clusters these on her bathroom counter or uses them to decorate a tea tray. But simple candles are easy to find at deep discounts and just as effective almost anywhere.

Try tucking scented votives or chunky columns into flowerpots, small bowls, or even hollowed out vegetables—or a wonderful variety of candlesticks can be found in discount stores, import shops, and even junk shops. They can be used as is, separately or in a cluster, or they can be painted or gilded. Snap up glass or crystal candlesticks whenever you see them; they are remarkably versatile decorating items, especially when adorned with crystals from chandeliers, glass beads, or silky tassels. Or create your own candlesticks using bits and pieces from the hardware store—wooden candle cups, pieces of turned doweling, and wood rosettes for bases.

Candles, too, lend themselves to creating a personal touch. If you have the time and inclination, you can make your own candles with molds and wicks, or you can decorate ready-made candles by carving with a warm knife, studding with small tacks or nails, or "decoupaging" with pressed flowers or leaves and melted paraffin. Yoli has even been known to spray-paint a set of tapers gold to match a table setting (she sprayed plastic fruit for a centerpiece), and they burned just fine!

A newer item we especially love are the little crystal bobeches available in gift stores. These slip down over a taper and give the effect of a little candle chandelier. You can also find little hurricane covers and miniature metal shades to dress up your candles.

Yet another source of lovely, soft light in many areas of your home is a set of tiny white twinkle lights. Small as they are, they emit a surprising amount of light. Try twining them around a banister, perhaps along with an ivy garland. Use them to circle a mirror or line a shelf. Hang them on your patio or under the umbrella of your patio table—and tangle them among the morning glories and trees for dinner under the stars. Or use them to line a window in your child's room—an instant starry nightlight.

However you choose to beautifully light your home, remember that all sources of light are also energy sources and can be hazardous.

Watch out for wires that could trip people or candles left burning in a room. Be especially careful with

Light is sweet, and it pleases the eyes to see the sun.

—The Book of Ecclesiastes

halogen lamps, which burn very hot and should be kept away from small children, pets, and all drapery or fabric. (*Never* drape a pink scarf over a halogen lamp!) It goes without saying that the wiring in your house should be inspected regularly and kept up to code.

But beyond these basic safety and design considerations, we say, let your light shine. Open the curtains to flood your rooms with cheerful sunlight, or fill in for the sun with soft candles, gentle lamps, clear and helpful task lights, even soft nightlights—and be creative with those "twinkles."

With all that light in your beautiful home, doesn't your life seem just a little brighter?

Bright Ideas

Shining Examples

Here are some ideas for creating your own lamps and shades.

BASIC BASES

☼ *A watering can*

☼ *A cookie jar or bean pot*

☼ *A teapot or coffeepot*

☼ *A wooden birdhouse*

☼ *A terra-cotta flowerpot or window box*

☼ *An old bottle wrapped with twine*

☼ *A child's wooden toy*

☼ *A miniature chair with a teddy bear sitting on it*

☼ *Old sports equipment—football helmet, base-ball bat, etc.*

☼ *A large bowling trophy*

☼ *A chunk of driftwood or hollowed piece of log*

☼ *A beat-up manual typewriter*

☼ *A stack of books (attached with brackets, brass rod up back)*

✿ An old can with antique label

✿ A figurine (animal, vegetable, or lighthouse!)

✿ A "Choo-Choo" bag from the sixties

✿ A pair of cowboy boots

SHADY IDEAS

✿ Autumn leaves—real or silk (Arrange on watercolor paper, cover with clear plastic.)

✿ Silk flowers or butterflies (Attach to shades with glue gun.)

✿ Pierced paper (Fit watercolor paper over purchased shade. Use large needle to create pierced design.)

✿ Buttons or bows (Just glue onto purchased shades.)

✿ An old chenille bedspread (Trim with fringe or pom-poms.)

✿ Antique linens (Gather around purchased shade or glue onto wire form.)

✿ A monogrammed towel (Cut so monogram shows.)

✿ Black lace on a fabric background (Trim with matching fringe.)

- ✿ Children's artwork (Laminate and glue onto form or paper shade.)
- ✿ Beads (String on wire and wrap around lamp form.)
- ✿ Stencil or stamp a ready-made fabric or paper shade.

10

Window Treats

Easy and Fabulous Curtains, Drapes, and More

NOTHING COULD BE MORE SIMPLE or more beautiful than a sparkling pane of glass overlooking a private garden or a woodland countryside. Nothing could grace a room more beautifully than an interesting old window framed by graceful wooden molding. In other words, you don't even need window treatments in your beautiful home ... unless your window happens to be a squat little square, the afternoon sun glares in uncomfortably, a draft from the window makes you shiver, or you'd rather not have passersby glancing in at you. But even if cosmetic concerns, lighting, insulation, or privacy are not considerations, a well-chosen drape or curtain, shutter or blind, window scarf or window hanging can do a lot to enhance a window's beauty. For most of us, creating a beautiful home on a budget will include some form of window decor.

The good news is that it's never been easier to adorn windows with very little investment of time and money. No-sew options abound, as do wonderful low-cost alternatives.

What do you do with a window?

Curtains and drapes, of course, are the most traditional form of window dressing, and these range from simple gathered or pleated panels to elaborate lined treatments complete with cornices or valances. Curtain alternatives include blinds or window shades, used alone or in combination with curtains or "toppers" of some kind.

All of these treatments, in their traditional forms, require a considerable investment of money, time, sewing skill, or all three. But several strategies can reduce your investment while maintaining a rich look.

One useful strategy for covering your windows is to combine basic coverings from a discount source with an eye-catching, rich-looking accent. Inexpensive sheer panels can look fabulous teamed with a decorator rod and a valance crafted from beautiful old linens. Plain miniblinds can retreat modestly under a rich swag-and-jabot treatment created by draping decorator fabric over window-scarf rings from the fabric store. Bargain-basement curtains and shades can be stenciled with fabric paint, decorated with glued-on trim, caught up with handcrafted tiebacks, hung by sewn-on ribbons, or even dressed up by decorative stenciling on the wall around them. Rich, billowy fabrics can disguise very simple construction and inexpensive hardware.

Whatever your strategy, ingenuity and innovative hardware can take you a long way. In fact, we recommend that as a first step you visit a fabric or hardware store to see what is available for low-cost window dressing. You may be amazed to see the cut-to-size, easy-to-cover foam cornice boards, the fusible tapes that provide almost instant hems and pleated headings, the kits for creating roll-up shades, the specialty rods and brackets that make it easy to create swags, festoons, jabots, and other fancy touches. The store may even provide how-to videos to show you how to use these inexpensive tools.

You don't really need specialty tools or hardware, however, to hang a simple, no-sew treatment. All you need is a length of interesting fabric, some simple hardware, and some imagination.

Yoli, for instance, created a valance for her kitchen using bright tea towels, some cup hooks, and some miniature baskets from the craft store. She simply tacked the curtains together to form a continuous strip, hung the baskets from the corners and center of the window top, and draped the towels through the handles of the baskets. In another home, she draped the towels through the center of antique crystal drawer pulls (the long kind that attach to the cabinet in two places).

Our friend Anne used a similar strategy to top her plain curtains for the Christmas season. Using a length of green and red plaid from a sale table at the fabric store, she draped it across the top of her curtains and held it in place with dime-store Della Robbia candle rings. The result was a plaid swag topper accented by little wreaths. She didn't even hem the ends of the fabric!

For an even simpler but highly effective treatment, try hanging plain little plastic rings from cuphooks at the tops of your windows. A length of lightweight fabric can then be run through the rings, knotted and puffed around them if you wish, then allowed to dangle at the sides like a swag. For more interest, you can knot the ends or use rubber bands to create a series of poufs. You can also use napkin rings of any design to puff your fabric through.

You don't even need a curtain rod to hang your curtains. Why not paint a tree branch gold or black and use it to hang tab-top drapes? Put a bamboo pole into service to hang nubby-cotton cafe curtains. Attach ribbon-top curtains to oars or pool cues. Or just staple fabric into place atop a window and cover the staples with a wide ribbon, a grapevine swag, a drape of fabric, or a pediment from an old, broken piece of furniture.

The basic rule of thinking function, not furniture, is especially handy when it comes to window treatments. Instead of assuming, "I need curtains or blinds," try to think, "I need a way to maintain privacy while letting the light in," "I would like to dress up this beautiful window molding and tie the windows in with the rest of the room," or "I need insulation to keep the heat in this winter." You may find that a lace tablecloth threaded on a thin pole answers your first need, a fringed shawl draped over a commercial windowscarf holder answers the second, and a rich quilted fabric sewn into a Roman shade (or created with iron-on Roman shade tape) answers the third.

Don't overlook the possibility of using window treatments to disguise flaws in your room or change the overall proportions. It's easy to alter the apparent width and length of a window by installing curtain rods a little higher or wider than the window opening, although this trick does work a little better with lined treatments. A charmless metal window can be transformed into an arch, with fabric shirred above it on a curved rod, or rendered practically invisible with a simple shade that matches the wall color.

Creative window dressing should not be limited to window coverings, however. A windowsill or even a sash can become a miniature display shelf, perfect for displaying items that love the light—especially glass and plants. Weathered shutters and a window box hung indoors around the window can add a welcome touch of whimsy. Wooden shelves mounted on hardware-store corbels over a window can combine window decoration with display space. A simple coat of paint in a contrasting color can be all you need to play up an interesting window frame—or a frameless window can be framed with a stamped or stenciled vine, an eye-catching wallpaper border, or a freehand design.

Consider using the window itself as display space—a sunny backdrop for a stained-glass medallion, a collection of miniature pitchers, or a nylon banner. Crystals from old chandeliers hanging on silk cords in a bright window will cast beautiful prisms around a room, and inexpensive teacups hanging from plastic suction cups will add a touch of cheer. Or try painting a slab of wood with designs on both sides (or ask a crafty friend to do it) and hang it by chains in a prominent window.

For a truly unique warm-weather window treatment, try painting your window screens or screen doors. Simply mask the edges of the screen, lay on

> *Windows are the smiles of the house.*
>
> —Emily Post

newspaper, and paint with acrylic craft paint thinned with water. (Practice first on an old screen or a piece of screening.) The effect will be subtle but interesting, a delicate design or a wash of color that fades in and out of view with the change of light.

Whatever window treatment or technique you opt for, remember that a window is part of a room's total decor. It should fit the room in color and fabric and style, either drawing the eye as an accent or blending harmoniously into the background. A print used in a valance should appear again in a pillow or a slipcover; an unusual texture should echo somewhere else in the room.

And don't overlook the possibility of changing your window coverings seasonally. In winter or blazing summer, lined drapes may keep your utility bills low. But during seasons where you want to open your windows to the breeze, why not hang sheers or lace on tension rods and disguise the drapery hardware with a swath of tulle?

Season by season, looking in or looking out, the total effect will be nothing but beautiful.

Bright Ideas

13 Lucky Ideas for
Dressing Your Windows

❀ Stretch sheer fabric across window, securing top and bottom with staples, and tie once in the middle to make an hourglass. Cover staples with ribbon or trim.

❀ Attach clip-on metal curtain rings to colorful tea towels or (for a bathroom) terry bath towels; hang from a tension rod.

❀ The quickest: Run an inexpensive curtain rod through the hem of a sheet (or sheets), hang and tie back with an interesting cord or ribbon, silk ivy, or colorful cotton bandannas. Or make a "bishop's sleeve" using rubber bands or plastic twist ties.

❀ Drape a series of vintage hankies, napkins, doilies, or tea towels at an angle (points down) over a valance rod or just over the top of curtain panels. Tack together with basting stitches to hold in place and attach tiny tassels, even beaded earrings or old crystals from a chandelier, to decorate the points.

❁ Use a kit to fuse fabric or wallpaper onto a roll-up shade.

❁ Thread a brass cafe rod through the edges of a lace tablecloth and hang. Drape more lace over the top like a window scarf—or a calico print or checked tablecloth for contrast.

❁ Hem a length of sheer fabric. Staple in gathers beneath an old dresser crown (from a broken piece of furniture) or a wooden pediment from an architectural or hardware store. Nail above the window so the pediment forms a cornice and the fabric hangs as a curtain.

❁ Hand-drape a billowing length of tulle, gauze, or other filmy fabric around a curtain or valance rod. Wrap around as many times as you want, allowing the fabric to fall in billowing loops, then let it hang down at the sides. Decorate by tucking baby's breath into the folds. Or wind a silk cord with the fabric and let it fall down into tassels at the end.

❁ Drape a long scarf through rings to form a silky valance. Or sew ribbons at intervals to the long side of the scarf and tie over a rod to make a tie-top valance.

❁ Use a grommet punch (available from fabric or hardware stores) to insert metal eyelets along the top of a hemmed length of heavy fabric.

Run a length of rope through the eyelets and over a curtain rod to hang, or thread a thin rod directly through the holes. For an even simpler treatment, just hang the eyelets over nails at the top of the curtain.

❈ Disguise a truly ugly view (the dumpster in the alley?) by setting a decorative screen in front of the bare window.

❈ Stiffen a piece of fabric with iron-on interfacing, cut into a decorative shape (points, scallops, etc.), glue on trim, and staple to top of window to make a tailored valance. Disguise staples with ribbon or a piece of molding.

❈ Sew a simple rod pocket at the top of two fringed chenille bedspreads. Hang on a curtain rod and tie back with matching ball fringe. For a different look, try Indian bedspreads from an import store.

Decking the Walls

Using Your Big Canvas

WHAT CAN YOU DO with a big, bare wall?

The possibilities are almost endless. Think of your walls as a big, wonderful canvas for your most exquisite, most creative decorative art.

Needless to say, you can hang pictures on a wall—large and small, fine art, dime-store prints, your children's art, or even your own creation. You can cover it with wallpaper, fabric, cork tiles, or even a bamboo shade. You can use it as a backdrop for a dramatic vignette—a glass shelf resting on two wooden corbels, an antique chair, a draped mirror, and a bust. You can back furniture up against it—a sofa, chair, armoire—or line it with shelves or bookcases.

And of course you can paint it—again and again—with pale or bright or glossy or texturized paint, transforming the look and the feel of a room for a very minimal investment of money and time.

Paint is a proven room-brightener even for paneled rooms. Emilie learned this firsthand a few years back when she first mustered the courage to paint and paper her guest room. The converted barn where she lives was walled throughout with distinctive barnwood paneling, and although she loved the effect, she wanted a lighter feel for her romantic "Princess Room." She held off for years, however, reluctant to paint over the paneling. When she finally did it—primed the paneling, painted it white, and papered the top half of the room—what a transformation! The rustic feel remained, but the overall flavor of the room was pure feminine romance. Emilie was so pleased with the effect that she went on to paint the dark ceiling in her bedroom white.

The most wonderful thing about paint as transforming agent is that it is such an inexpensive investment—so inexpensive that you can afford to play with it. Why not experiment with interesting color schemes and effects? You can always paint over anything you don't like!

Instead of just rolling a coat of paint on a wall, for instance, try sponging or combing effects. Stamp or stencil a design around the ceiling, or use stamps to create a mock wallpaper. Paint one wall (or all four) a different color, or mimic wainscoting by painting the bottom half of a room a contrasting color and installing a chair rail where the colors meet. While you're at it, paint the trim in the room a crisp white or a vivid contrasting color.

For truly original walls, steel your nerve, grab your paintbrush, and try some freehand designs. With a wide brush, paint a wavy border around the ceiling line, then tie your line in a bow over a window or door. Paint simple folk-art designs (apples, flowers) at intervals above a chair rail, or even cover a wall with a colorful mural.

And don't forget doors and ceilings. They, too, can be painted, stenciled, sponged, or decorated. (How about a blue ceiling decorated with a moon and stars?) Even the knobs on cabinets or the tiles in a bathroom or kitchen can be adorned with a few swipes of your paintbrush.

As an alternative to painting your walls, of course, you can cover them with wallpaper or fabric. Papering a wall takes a bit of care but is not really hard, and even discount stores offer plenty of designs to choose from. If you've never papered a wall before, we suggest you start with a simple all-over random pattern (to avoid alignment problems) and a small room such as a bathroom.

As an alternative to covering a wall with paper, you can use a wallpaper border on a painted wall. This works especially well around the ceiling line, above a chair rail, or around windows or fireplaces. Or you can cut out motifs from a wallpaper pattern and apply them individually or in groups. A large motif from a pictorial wallpaper could work as a wall mural, framed by strips of molding. A series of small motifs or a long cutout vine can beautifully frame a window.

For a striking effect, why not use matching paper to line a glass-covered cabinet?

Fabric, too, covers walls beautifully. It can be pasted on like wallpaper, using powdered cellulose or a premixed vinyl paste. It can be stapled onto a padded wall, shirred on a rod or cord, and hung from the ceiling, or simply shirred and stapled directly on the wall. Even ceilings can be covered with fabric, although this gravity-defying process may require an assistant. (Actually, a partner comes in handy for covering walls as well.)

Your options for wallcovering, of course, include more than paint, wallpaper, and fabric. When Emilie was a newlywed, she textured a wall in her dining room by nailing paper egg cartons to the wall and painting over them! For a similarly eye-catching treatment, try covering a wall with cork tiles, mirror tiles, angled paneling, even a bamboo window shade. You can decoupage a small area with magazine covers, sheet music, wallpaper motifs—you name it. You can apply wooden molding to the wall as a chair rail or ceiling molding or even to mimic architectural features. Textured motifs can be glued on around a fireplace or bookcases. Use your imagination, but keep in mind that many of these alternative coverings may be hard to undo without resurfacing the wall.

Once you've painted or papered or covered your walls, of course—unless you painted a mural—you still have a wall to decorate.

Here, too, fortunately, the possibilities are endless and the budget can be quite small. The fact is that almost anything can become a wall decoration by the simple act of being hung on a wall! In the early days of our marriages, we did just that—scouting garage sales, flea markets, and charity stores for interestingly shaped objects that could double as wall decor. We would go *behind* the charity stores, pick out rejected items, and hang them on the wall.

Paintings, prints, and photographs are the classic wall decorations, and unless you are an investor, these can often be found for very little money at import stores, discount stores, craft sales, and the like. Look for items that express something of who you are. Yoli's husband, Bob, for example, has decorated the walls of his office with a series of ten *Sports Illustrated* covers inexpensively housed in Lucite box frames. Emilie's husband (also a Bob), expresses his interest in history by hanging old tools and magazine prints. A wall of photos would be a natural expression of what you love (for a museum look, try black-and-white photos with wide white mats and thin black frames); so would an arrangement of calendar prints from a place you love to visit.

You may find, in fact, that the real challenge of finding something to put on the wall comes not with the picture, but with the frame. When you can, look for items that are already framed, that require no frame, or that you can frame yourself for very little. A great-looking poster, for example, can look great in an inexpensive glass or metal poster frame from the hobby store. A striking photograph can be mounted under a ready-cut white mat and framed with inexpensive framing clips. An interesting note card may fit neatly in a dime-store frame that you have painted or touched up with a gold-paint pen or padded and covered with fabric.

Pictures don't always need to be framed, of course. Try mounting an inexpensive print on a tray or a piece of board and covering the edges with ribbon or fabric trim. Oil or acrylic paintings on canvas can be especially effective when left unframed, and you can glue ribbon or rope around the edges of the stretcher frame if the raw look bothers you.

If you think you can't afford a painting on canvas, think again. Interesting old oils can often be found in antique stores or flea markets. A talented friend might be talked into creating one for you. Or you can even make your own painting on a large stretched canvas from an art supply shop. You don't have to paint a masterpiece. You can roll on stripes in different colors, stencil or stamp a design, or even just paint the canvas a solid color to contrast with your room.

An interesting alternative to a painting without a frame is a frame without a painting. If you see a great-looking frame (old or new) at a bargain price, try hanging it on the wall just as it is—or hang something cute on the wall inside the frame—a smaller picture, a hat, a mirror, even a toy or a fan.

An important exception to the cheap-framing principle is a fine-art quality print or painting or photograph that you plan to keep a long time. (This would include precious family photographs.) Inexpensive framing techniques usually include materials that, over time, would hasten the deterioration of the art. This doesn't mean you need to seal your art in a museum case, but you should have it professionally framed with acid-free materials. Photos and prints should always be matted to prevent their adhering to glass. And if you want to display precious old family photos, have copies made at a local print or photo shop. Store the originals safely away and use the copies to deck your walls.

Traditional forms of "art," of course, are far from your only options for wall decoration. Anything from a trivet to a tray will serve; in fact, an arrangement of objects with varying shapes and sizes can be especially effective. Sconces and other wall-hung lighting fixtures can combine with mirrors, paintings, and photographs. Odd shapes can hang among squared-off framed pictures. A little shelf or cabinet can combine with a mirror or a group of plates in an eye-catching vignette. A whole gallery of family photos can smile from a variety of wooden and metal and even ceramic frames.

An effective wall grouping usually works best with bigger items in the center and smaller items added around the edges; this kind of arrangement is also easier to put together. If you are uneasy with the "eyeball and hammer" method of alignment, try making a paper pattern of each piece and moving them around on the floor until you have a general feel for how they could be arranged. This is another case where working with a friend is much easier: one of you can hold up the pictures, the other can stand back and pass judgment.

Tradition says that pictures (and other wall decorations) should be hung at about eye level, but the very existence of this tradition means that you can really make a statement by breaking it! Try hanging a picture higher or lower than expected—high over a bookcase, for example, or behind a lamp table on a level with the lamp base. Or try combining wall-hung decorations with items on the floor—for example, a little shelf and a small picture can cluster with a plant or topiary, or a Raggedy Ann doll in a child's rocking chair can enjoy her own eye-level miniature painting.

Yet another possibility is not to hang a piece of art at all. Set it on a shelf or table and just let it lean against the wall. Emilie's son, Brad, and his wife, Maria, have created a truly wonderful family-photo

A great many people enjoy having taste but too few of them enjoy the things they have taste about.

—Russell Lyons

arrangement in their hallway without hanging a single picture. Instead, they have installed three wall-hung shelves and then filled them with a bevy of black-and-white family photos in assorted frames. Old family pictures (including Emilie's wedding picture) rub elbows with black-and-white candids of the children. No one visits Brad and Maria's home without a favorable comment on their fresh and interesting photo display.

Of course you don't always have to go for an unusual placement or grouping. A single, simple over-sized picture or hanging can make its own stunning statement. So can a matched set of botanical prints or a group of black-and-white photos lined up over a table in identical frames.

Being creative doesn't necessarily mean ignoring ideas that have proven effective through the years.

However you decide to deck your walls, remember to do it throughout your house. Don't neglect to decorate the walls of your kitchen and bathroom, your hallways, and even your utility rooms or garage! Sturdy, weatherproof wall hangings, plaques, or posters in frames can even find a home on your patio or porch.

Wherever you find an empty expanse of wall, consider it your opportunity to have fun and make your home more interesting and inviting. It's a wonderful opportunity to add a few more "brush strokes" to that beautiful work in progress—your home.

Bright Ideas

Suitable for Framing

Any of these items can be framed as a wall decoration . . . or just hang on the wall as they are!

- ✺ Small carved pieces from furniture or buildings
- ✺ Old windows—hang glass, curtains, and all!
- ✺ Interesting old letters or postcards
- ✺ Doors, shutters, or gates—the more beat-up the better!
- ✺ A glass shelf resting on wood or plaster corbels
- ✺ Children's artwork
- ✺ Photos (formal or candid)
- ✺ Interesting note cards
- ✺ Hats
- ✺ Upholstery remnants
- ✺ Antique doilies or handkerchiefs
- ✺ An unframed oil painting on stretched canvas (If you like, cover raw edges with velvet ribbon.)
- ✺ Seashells from the beach
- ✺ Tools with interesting shapes

❁ *Fans*

❁ *Sports equipment*

❁ *Quilts, afghans, or throws*

❁ *Vintage ceiling tins (Paint, hang in groups, use to frame a mirror or print.)*

❁ *Clocks*

❁ *Trays (Hang with cord or rest on little nails.)*

❁ *Tiles*

❁ *Trivets*

❁ *Tools of any kind: cutlery, farm implements, crochet hooks*

❁ *Musical instruments*

❁ *Architectural drawings and blueprints*

❁ *A chair (doubles as a small shelf!)*

❁ *Bunch of dried flowers with big ribbon hanging down—or eucalyptus, branches, twigs, wheat stalks.*

❁ *Grapevine arrangements*

❁ *Small cabinets*

❁ *Wreaths*

❁ *Magazine covers*

❁ *Plaster decorations from a paint-it-yourself store*

PAINT TRY-OUTS

Paint is a wonderful way to transform your walls, but it's hard to tell from a little paint chip how a given color will work in a given spot of your home. To avoid expensive mistakes, purchase a small can of the color you have in mind and use it to paint a large piece of plywood (at least three feet square). Place your plywood against the wall and observe the way the color works under different lighting conditions and with other colors in your home. If you are too impatient to try this, at least remember that paints tend to look darker on walls than they do on samples, so purchase a shade lighter than you think you need.

A Lifelong Journey

Emilie's Decorating Story

I DON'T REALLY THINK OF MYSELF as a decorator. I spent the first half of my grown-up life as a homemaker and mother, the second half running a business with my husband. Yet the home that Bob and I decorated together has been a stop on more than one city-wide home tour. It has even been featured in *Better Homes and Gardens.* (Yoli did the styling for the photo layouts!)

How did I get to this point? Simply by wanting to shape a home that was beautiful to look at and easy to live in . . . for everyone in our family.

As a child bride of 17, 1 began my decorating journey with almost nothing. In those early days I was trying to create a beautiful home on no budget at all! Learning to love what I had and to see the decorating potential in almost anything was pure necessity.

In those days, Bob and I eagerly accepted castoffs and hand-me-downs and wracked our brains for ways to transform these mismatched basics into a cozy, welcoming home. We spray-painted an old wrought-iron garden table for our kitchen. We moved the same little potted plants from kitchen to living room to bedroom. We rooted around behind charity shops for interesting discards we could hang on the walls in place of the art we didn't own.

Without knowing it, we were learning valuable lessons in loving and decorating with what we had. And with each house, we learned a little more about who we are, what we love, and how we can share ourselves by sharing our home.

We almost never had money for a decorator, but we always had our eyes open. I was constantly poring through magazines, looking for ideas that would work in our home. I sought ideas from friends and gathered inspiration from homes I visited. And I learned that "creative stealing" can be as valuable as "creative seeing" when it comes to decorating genius. In fact, the very act of adapting ideas from books and magazines, friends and acquaintances, seems to stimulate my own creativity. (I'm always eager to give credit and pass along my own ideas!)

I have to stress that the beauty and interest of our decorating is due as much to my husband's taste as my own. Not only is my Bob the gardener in our home, the one who furnishes the lush green lawn as well as flowers for indoors and out, but he is also the source of some of our most inventive decorating ideas. We have sometimes had to work a bit to marry his tastes with mine—his love of old farm tools, crumbling old books, and vintage signs with my passion for beautiful china, silver, and lovely old lace—but the result has been pleasing for both of us. Our home is our mutual work of art, and I look forward to many more years of its ongoing creation.

12

Beauty Underfoot

Improving Your Home's Bottom Line

YOU DON'T ALWAYS NEED a carpet! You don't even need a rug.

What you need is a beautiful place to set your feet . . . and to tie the rest of your room together.

Now, it may be that a rug is the way to go. If you live in a cool climate, you may need a soft floor covering for warmth. If you do a lot of aerobics, have a bad back, or always seem to end up lying on the floor to watch TV, the cushioning may be a kindness. A lovely rug from an antiques mart or even a discount store may be just the look to tie your conversational area together. (When Emilie decorated her great room, she spent the bulk of her decorating budget on a custom-dyed carpet that picked up the colors in her couch.) And for pure sensual comfort, a plush carpet underfoot can be a delight.

But alternately, consider the joys of a cool, shining, hardwood floor, all bare or punctuated with beautiful small rugs.

Consider the drama of a shining, polished cement floor, a gleaming contrast to the softness of your upholstery.

Consider the interesting alternatives of brick, tile, or even sisal matting.

With a bit of creativity and a willingness to think beyond the obvious, the floors in your home can make a wonderful, unforgettable statement.

If you live in a rental home, of course, or if your carpets are good and your budget small, your best option may be to build on what you have. Bright area rugs can define your living areas. Colorful rag rugs can decorate not only the odd corner, but also walls and furniture. (Try crocheting a rag rug out of denim strips cut from old jeans!) You can simply let the carpets be themselves and integrate them into the room by using fabrics, wall color, and accessories. In some cases you may find it works perfectly well simply to ignore the carpets and draw the eye away from them.

If you have the freedom to install your own carpeting, we do encourage you to dream beyond basic beige. Your floors can provide the thread of pure color that unifies a home. Try a lovely slate gray, a medium blue, a rosy salmon, or an outdoorsy green—then play up different aspects of that base color throughout your home.

Or then again, you might want to pull up all the carpets and polish the floor—even if it's cement. Cement floors can be painted in a variety of colors.

(Try applying paint with a broom for a textured effect, or applying a burnt-umber wash over a base color for an antique look.) Once painted, the concrete surface can be protected with polyurethane or even polished to a shine. The cost is surprisingly low when compared to that of wall-to-wall carpet, the upkeep is minimal, the look is clean and interesting . . . and if you want to, you can skate on your floors!

Yoli's neighbors, the Wilsons, created a dramatic statement in their home by painting their cement floors shiny black and continuing a black-and-white motif throughout the house. The walls and upholstery are all white and the large coffee table is black, accented with gold fleur de lis, and topped with an oversized clear vase holding lemons and limes or white gladiolus. An arrangement of black-and-white photos adorns one wall, some white plaster urns filled with palms fill a corner. The overall effect is stunning yet surprisingly livable.

Wood floors, too, can be transformed with a little imagination. Left to itself, of course, a houseful of gleaming wood underfoot can be stunning. But there is no law that says you have to finish wood floors in a natural wood color. They can be stained or painted (try a bright blue or a battleship gray) or whitewashed and stenciled. Any painting technique you use for walls—combing, sponging, stamping—can work for floors as well. Try stenciling a border of leaves and flowers around the edge of a room—or how about a large checkerboard pattern applied with sponges or stamps? Just be sure to remove any old wax or varnish and sand lightly before applying paint. When you are through, a hard-working coat of polyurethane will protect your finish.

The option of painting your wood floors is especially attractive if the floors are damaged or worn. The cost of sanding and refinishing floors can be high, and the process can be time-consuming and disruptive. Painting your floors can be a low-cost but quite effective substitute.

Whether painted or polished, concrete or wood, bare floors lend themselves naturally to a variety of decorative effects. If you have the skill, you can even paint area rugs directly on your floor. An oblong or oval design painted directly on the floor becomes a kind of permanent area rug—a true conversation piece, and it never needs washing.

For a temporary floor covering in the summer, try a painted canvas floor cloth. Simply hem a piece of heavy canvas, paint or stencil in the design you want with acrylic paint, then seal with shellac or varnish. (Be sure to place newspaper under the cloth while you're working, and paint in a well-ventilated area.) Once dry, these cloths are extremely durable. They can be rolled up and stored when not in use, and the edges can even be cut into scallops or points. If you like the way they look, try painting a sisal floor mat.

And while you're at it, why not stencil the risers on your stairway? Try painting the names of your children, or imitate the look of a sampler with different designs on each riser. Leaves, flowers, animals, butterflies—all could lend a touch of distinction and a spark of interest to your stairway. Small areas of your home such as entranceways, alcoves, and even bathrooms offer you the opportunity to try more unusual treatments for a minimal price. Try paving just a small area with cool ceramic tile, mosaic, or even the new veneer bricks (these very thin bricks apply just like tile). A floor finish that might be time- or cost-prohibitive in a large room might be just what you need in a tiny one.

The bottom line is: you don't need a king's ransom to decorate your floors. With a little ingenuity, even the underfoot areas of your home can be hospitable, warm, cozy . . . and beautiful.

Duty makes us do things well, but love makes us do them beautifully.

—Phillip Brooks

13

Room for Living

Establishing Cozy Common Areas

WHERE IN YOUR HOUSE does everyone love to gather?

It may be a big country kitchen or a breezy patio, but more likely it's a living room, family room, or den, a place where family members come together to talk or read or play games or (let's face it) watch TV.

Contrary to what some people think, such a room does not have to be worn or shabby or dumpy to be comfortable and inviting.

And where in your house do you invite your guests for conversation? For many of us in these casual days, the same rooms serve—or you may have separate, more formal rooms for entertaining and special occasions. But even if you prefer the style of elegant parlors and sitting rooms, all of these "receiving" areas should be hospitable and comfortable as well as beautiful and impressive.

Regardless of your floor plan, in other words, the "sitting rooms" where family and guests gather are truly the heart of your home, and they deserve your best efforts to make them both beautiful and cozy. Besides, these are the rooms where everyone will see and appreciate what you've done!

What do you do with a sitting room or other common space? The specific furnishings, lighting, and accessories in a living room or family room will vary according to what you have and what you like, but any common area is likely to require the following components.

Somewhere to Sit

We hope you realize by now that you don't necessarily need a sofa and loveseat flanking a coffee table. What you need in a common area is furniture that promotes commonality—something that beckons people to draw close to one another and allows them to converse comfortably.

There's nothing wrong with a sofa or futon, of course, especially if you like to relax by lying down. You may even decide you want a roomful of sofas. But a cozy little conversational group of chairs with ottomans may serve your purpose just as well. So may a gathering of mismatched rocking chairs circling the hearth.

You can even bring in furniture from the garden for a fresh kind of comfort. Wooden Adirondack chairs and footstools painted in unexpected patterns and softened with a bevy of cushions can make a unique statement—try painting the wooden slats in different primary colors, or add gold accents to a chair painted glossy black. Metal or resin lawn furniture—or even wrought iron—can add a similar fresh look and inexpensive extra seating at the same time. There's no law, in fact, that says you can't enjoy a "glider" or swing indoors (as long as the ceiling joists hold).

Whatever your seating, use your decorating savvy to make it cute as well as serviceable. Slipcover it in gorgeous fabrics, dress it up with pillows, brighten it with a fuzzy throw, or even drape a colorful rag rug over the back for a textural surprise. Use your paintbrush and your fabric box to transform inexpensive director's chairs or even metal folding chairs into eye-pleasing extra seating.

Somewhere to Put Your Feet

Be honest! It's hard to get really cozy in a sitting room unless you can put your feet up. That's why ottomans and footstools add so tremendously to the comfort of your common rooms. And these wonderful little underfoot items offer a decorating bonanza. Not only do they provide additional seating and easy-to-make decorative accents; they are also simple and quick to paint or slipcover, and they often can be found for very little money.

Even a pricey antique store may have a unique little footstool lurking in a corner for an affordable price. Your local discount store or a garage sale may offer you a "transformable" ottoman for almost nothing. And you'll be surprised what a strong statement such a diminutive piece of furniture can make.

For an elegant and easy footstool makeover try sewing multicolored remnants of velvet together in a random pattern like a Victorian crazy quilt. (If you wish, add traditional "feather" stitching.) When you've put together a big enough "quilt," staple it over the footstool's existing padding, trim the edges, and tuck them under.

For an even easier transformation of a round rolling ottoman from a discount store, simply gather a circle of fabric around the edges. You'll have a little "shower cap" that fits easily around the ottoman—just tighten the gathering stitches and tie them. If you don't want to sew, simply drape the fabric, tuck it under, and staple in place. A more contemporary Parson's-type ottoman can also be covered with stapled fabric. An unfinished piece of needlepoint rescued from a garage sale may offer just enough yardage to top an unfinished footstool from a craft store.

For a different approach, try drafting non-footstool items into footstool duty. A child's chair, hand-painted in whimsical patterns, can serve either as a low table or a place to rest your feet. So can a sturdy wooden box, as is or with a cushion. Even a stack of boxy floor cushions can serve this purpose, inviting friends and family to make themselves comfortable in your beautiful home.

Somewhere to Put Your Teacup

You may not need a coffee table, but you do need some flat surfaces in a common room to hold lamps, drinks, reading material, and decorative objects. A grouping of small tables in interesting shapes and varying heights might serve this purpose. (Try unstacking a set of stacking tables and spreading them out.) A piano bench, a butler's tray, a rolling tea cart, a wicker nightstand, or a beautifully painted wooden tray perched on an ottoman could also work. Old trunks are familiar stand-ins for tables, and stacks of old suitcases are becoming a newer standard. Instead of a traditional sofa table behind a sofa, try stacking two garden benches—or simply use a row of extra chairs from the dining room.

Then again, you might want a coffee table! Something gleaming and oversized can beautifully center a conversational grouping—holding not only your books and your tea tray but an eye-catching collection or a beautiful floral arrangement.

An extra old wooden dining table can serve admirably in this capacity—either cut down the legs or replace them with a base from the hardware store. If the wood is beautiful, just polish it and let it gleam. If the surface is scarred and ugly, try painting and stenciling it, or just drape it with a beautiful cloth.

Glass-topped garage-sale finds can become lovely sitting room treasures with just a little work. A black/green verdigris finish can transform the look of a standard-issue metal-framed table. Or a wood table with glass inlay can become an eye-catching tile-topped table. Just replace the glass with a sheet of plywood and use tile adhesive to apply the ceramic design of your choice.

When searching for side tables and coffee tables in your sitting areas, always be on the lookout for parts that can be put together beautifully. A tacky, nondescript, iron base you find on the street can be topped with a butcher block, an old door, a window, or a thick pane of glass to create an interesting table. An antique sewing machine base could serve as a table base. So could a set of sawhorses or an antique ironing board. Here, as in all your decorating, your creativity will make your room both affordable and distinctive.

Something to Make You Comfy

There are a few times in life—and in decorating—where you may choose to sacrifice comfort for the sake of beauty. We believe those times should be very few.

It's just not that hard to add those little details that make a room invitingly cozy as well as pleasing to the eye.

In particular, cushioned surfaces add to that air of cozy comfort. Plenty of soft, comfy pillows add a touch of luxury to any home and a decorative flourish to any sitting room. Use them with abandon on your sitting pieces—some in a print to match the curtains, some in a contrasting variety of patterns, some soft and inviting, some clearly just for show. Be sure, however, to leave enough space for people to actually sit. If you love a pile of pillows on every surface, consider providing a big basket to hold them while people are occupying those surfaces!

If your family is the kind that likes to lie on the floor, soft rugs and floor pillows are a wise comfort investment. Try stacking a group of these together when not in use and tying together like a package with a big ribbon—or nestling them together under an end table.

And pillows aren't the only kind of comforting detail in a room. We also like to make sure that any common room has something to snuggle under. A pile of folded afghans or lap quilts under a library table or a woolen throw draped like a scarf over a wingback chair provides a warm accent as well as a source of actual warmth. Your family and even your guests will never feel so at home as when you've snuggled them up on the couch with a puffy pillow under their head

Other things being equal, comfort is the most important attribute of charm.

—Emily Post

and a cozy cotton or wool throw tucked in around them. Here, of course, is the place to display that gorgeous fisherman's afghan that your grandmother knitted or the woolen tartan throw you brought home from your trip to Nova Scotia. But resist the temptation just to fold a flame-stitched throw over the back of your sofa like your grandmother did. Instead, drape it over the arm of a chair, fold it and stack it with other throws under a table or on a trunk, drape it over a folk-art quilt rack, or simply hang from a brass and porcelain knob on the wall—a decorative accent easily at hand for snuggling.

Something to Do, Someplace to Do It, and Someplace to Put It

Any room where people gather will need to offer some accommodation for the activities they love to do when they gather.

This means that some common rooms will need a table and chairs for games, snacks, and puzzles. A simple card table and set of folding chairs can serve this purpose admirably. (Give them a new lease on life by removing the padded surfaces, covering them with wonderful fabric, and replacing them in their frames.) So can a painted breakfast set or a chrome kitchen table from the 1950s.

Shelving and cabinets, too, can be an important addition to your sitting rooms. For a set of unusual bookcases, try stacking five wooden garden benches, each painted a different color. An old stepladder, too, can hold a set of shelves—just rest shelving boards on the rungs. (A miniature stepladder can hold a mini-gallery of family portraits.)

Placed on their sides, any number of objects can serve as shelving: squared baskets, crates, terra-cotta plumbing pipes, even (we hesitate to say it) bricks and boards.

And don't be afraid to use standard commercial shelving of various kinds—either as is or spruced up with paint, molding, and fabric. If lined up together closely, a set of white melamine-coated bookshelves from the hardware center can mimic a set of built-ins, and simple crown molding glued around the edges will heighten that illusion. For a softer look, try curtaining a set of inexpensive bookshelves with draped fabric—staple at the top or hang from a rod, then tie back at the sides. Or go for a bit wilder look and place your books and knickknacks on standard metal utility shelving spray-painted in bright colors.

Audio and video equipment have become standard residents of most sitting rooms. These don't really need to be hidden; in fact, some ready-made media centers are quite attractive. If you wish, however, you can stow your electronics behind the beautiful doors of old cabinets, armoires, or even sideboards. Your standard-issue bookshelves may also offer the option of adding cabinet doors to stow your equipment—or you can add drapes or screens.

Exercise equipment, too—from exercise bikes to aerobics mats to steps and hand weights—often finds itself living in your common areas. This equipment can hide behind a screen or a curtain or be tucked into cabinets—or just allowed to be itself in an inconspicuous corner. A well-used exercise bike that you ride while watching TV deserves its place in your decor. A forlorn exercise bike that you use only as a coat rack, however, is nothing but an eyesore.

Something to Delight the Eye

Beauty, of course, is the last-but-not-least component in any common area.

At home amongst your comfortable seating, your cozy cushions, your practical footstools, tables, and shelves should reside items that catch the eye, delight the senses, and stimulate conversation.

Here is where your creativity and imagination shine—as you fill the walls, the tabletops, the floors, with your own special touch—the haunting, evocative silk-screen print you couldn't resist at the local college art show, the vignette you arrange so carefully in the corner (a plaster column, a graceful sculpture, an exuberant cascade of ivy), the population of dolls perched cheerfully in painted children's chairs, or even a wall arrangement of colorful puzzles you worked in this very room.

Decorating beautifully in your common rooms is really just a matter of remembering that you should always strive to nurture the spirit as well as to comfort the body. When you do that, you'll have a space where all the people you love . . . just love to be.

Bright Ideas

Ten Hat Tricks

Wondering where to hang your hat? Here are ten ideas for using hats beautifully:

✤ Hang as part of a vignette or wall arrangement—a straw garden hat hung with gardening tools and seed packets, an antique bonnet hung with little purse, fan, and antique photo.

✤ Hang as the "picture" inside an empty frame.

✤ Tilt rakishly on top of a lamp.

✤ Line up several hats over a window.

✤ Hang with its friends from a dime-store mug rack—or attach with clothespins to a line strung across a wall.

✤ Stack straw hats in a corner or on a table.

✤ Store in decorated Shaker boxes or old department store hatboxes, stack as a side table.

✤ Use to dress a collection of large dolls or stuffed animals.

✤ Decorate with silk flowers and hang on a door.

✤ Use an upside-down straw hat as a basket to hold a plant or even a crock of dip.

14

Sweet Sleeping

Creating a Place to Dream

IF YOU COUNT YOUR SLEEPING HOURS, the bedroom is the place in your home where you spend most of your time!

Of course, you do so much more than sleeping there. Your bedroom may also be your dressing room and reading room, your private retreat, your romantic hideaway. It only makes sense to focus your decorating efforts toward making it the most comfortable, beautiful place in your house.

What colors rest you and renew your spirit? Those are the colors you should choose for your sleeping chambers. Tradition calls for soft and cool colors in a bedroom, and we do love the idea of cool periwinkle walls iced with all-white accessories. But there is really no reason why your bedroom can't be red if that color works for you—although you might find a darker, bluer shade of red more restful than a screaming fire-engine shade. Any shade of pink, from rosy coral to cool lilac, will be especially flattering to the skin—an important consideration for a room where you may be caught without makeup!

A Spot to Snooze

Bedrooms are especially fun to furnish from flea markets and garage sales. (Even good wood furniture from many antique stores will be less expensive than new pieces from a furniture showroom.) Old bedsteads, chests of drawers, vanity tables, and all manner of other bargains can be transformed with paint, fabric, and imagination to create a lovely, restful haven. Look for old-fashioned high beds (or just headboards), wicker accessories, beautiful old mirrors, even interesting old drawer pulls—anything you can use to make your bedroom distinctive.

We would add an important caveat, however, to the matter of furnishing your bedroom from low-cost sources. Skimp on bedsteads, night tables, blanket boxes, accessories—but buy the very best mattress and box spring you can afford. Similarly, go for the bargains when it comes to storage pieces, but avoid anything whose drawers stick or catch (unless you know you can repair them). Saving money is simply not worth the price of a bad back or the daily irritation of wrestling with your furniture!

With this simple warning in mind, we urge you to have a wonderful time dreaming up the bedroom of your dreams! Old doors and shutters, for instance, make distinctive and fascinating headboards—just nail to the wall behind the bed. A section of old (or new) picket fencing can serve the same purpose, and lattice can also be cut with a small saw into a square or arched headboard shape. Or try soaking a tangle of grapevines from the hobby store until they are flexible and then shaping them into a dramatic arch behind the bed. (Echo the look by gluing twigs or grapevines around a dime-store mirror and perhaps some picture frames.)

An old iron bed frame is a real find in a junk or antique store. It will probably respond beautifully to a wire-brush scraping (to remove rust), a primer, and a coat or two of spray paint. Try red gloss enamel for a teenager's room or matte black with gold highlights (use that gold pen) for a sophisticated guest bedroom.

Don't be afraid to paint or decorate old wooden beds as well. If the wood is beautiful, you might want to have it stripped and refinished. If not, you can have fun with any number of decorative treatments. Use a crackle finish over a colored undercoat to create an instant antique with a subtle touch of color. Stencil a headboard to match a border around a window. Or pad an inexpensive headboard with batting and cover it with beautiful fabric you rescued from a remnant table.

You don't even need a headboard at all, in fact, to create a richly upholstered look around your bed. Instead of bothering with the headboard, just cover the wall behind the bed with fabric. Shirr the fabric and staple it for a romantic touch, or staple flat fabric over batting for a quilted look. You can even add little quilting "ties" at intervals with a large-eyed needle and pieces of contrasting yarn. Disguise the stapled edges of the fabric-covered area with painted lattice strips or molding, or simply glue on ribbon or fabric trim.

If you like the look of fabric around a bed, you can even go with a canopy look. This can be as simple as continuing your fabric wall treatment up over the top of the bed or as elaborate as attaching a wooden frame to the ceiling and hanging the drapery of your choice. Try draping lengths of sheer fabric from ceiling hooks (the kind used for hanging plants) or over painted dowel rods with screw-on finials hung at different heights over the bed.

For a dramatically romantic look with a minimum of effort, head for a camping or import store and buy a mosquito net. These nets consist of a circular frame hanging from a hook and a tent of gossamer netting hanging from the frame. To use as a bed treatment, simply attach the hook over the head of the bed so that the "tent" opening faces toward the foot. Open out the sides of the tent, pull them back, and attach them to the wall at the head of the bed. If you wish, you can decorate the hoop and the netting with garlands of silk greenery and flowers. You can take advantage of the net's tropical ambience and decorate with wicker, jungle prints, and safari furniture. Or just use the unadorned net as part of an all-white bedroom.

The bed, of course, is not the only piece of furniture in your bedroom, although it is by far the most important. In addition to a place to sleep, you need some kind of nightstand to hold your glasses, your book, and your alarm clock. You need adequate but soft lighting for reading in bed, and of course you need storage for your clothes and extra linens. You may also want a comfortable chair or two (for sitting or for laying out your clothes) and some sort of vanity or dressing table. Absolute musts are a mirror or two and, of course, something beautiful to look at. Fortunately, all of these furnishings can easily be yours with just a little bit of creativity.

Almost any small piece of furniture, for instance, can serve as a nightstand—and your nightstands don't need to match. Emilie's bed, for instance, is flanked by an antique coal scuttle (her husband, Bob's, nightstand) and a small oak table (her own nightstand). A tea cart of wood or wicker can make an adorable and useful nightstand. So can a set of wicker drawers in an iron frame, or even a piano bench. The old standby remedy of a cloth draped over a round side table from the dime store still works (try draping a sheer square over the top for an unusual effect). Or you can top an oversized architectural corbel with a heavy piece of glass for a dramatically different look.

The only thing to keep in mind regarding your nightstand is that it should be reasonably sturdy—to resist your nighttime stumblings and your sleepy slaps at the alarm clock. While a painted tray perched on a delicate stand may look appealing, you'll regret the choice every time you knock it over and send your glasses flying!

Bedside lighting should be kept soft and romantic—but also adequate for reading in bed. Swing-arm lamps mounted on the wall can be useful, as can floor lamps placed at the right height. If your decor is romantic, have fun with fringed silk or beaded lampshades. Or if you enjoy a vintage twenties or thirties

look, scour the secondhand shops for an old-fashioned bed lamp that attaches to your headboard.

Sleepytime Storage

The other furniture you use in your bedroom will
depend in part on how much storage space you need.
Armoires and other large storage pieces were invented
in the days when walk-in closets were unheard of, and
they can still serve the purpose of beautifully holding
your clothes. You can find them in antique stores and
sometimes in secondhand shops as well as unfinished
furniture stores. If you can't afford such a piece, you
can disguise a rolling clothes rack behind a folding
screen—or use a curtain to transform an odd alcove or
an entire end of a room into a "closet." Tall lingerie
chests, roomy trunks, or cedar chests also provide
valuable storage space if you need them—as do old-
fashioned tall beds, whose long dust ruffles can con-
ceal a number of storage boxes.

Another interesting solution to bedroom storage
needs is to store beautiful items in plain view. Hang
your hats on the wall in an interesting arrangement,
for instance, or drape costume chains and necklaces
from a series of decorative hooks. Even your everyday
clothing can become part of the decor if you install a
Shaker-style peg rail around the wall at chair-rail
height. You can hang all manner of items, from hats to
vintage clothing to your bathrobe, from this rail.

A peg rail is actually quite simple to make from
flat molding and ready-made pegs. Simply drill holes
at regular intervals along the molding using a bit that
is just smaller than the pegs. Then apply a dab of

wood glue to each peg and tap it in place with a hammer. Finish the rail any way you like (an old-fashioned distressed look is effective) and attach it to the wall with finishing nails.

If you love a vanity for holding your beauty accessories, look for a wonderful old one in an antique store. If your budget won't stretch that far, however, you can create a beautiful dressing table from a garage-sale castoff (those ubiquitous kidney-shaped tables!) or just a plywood top on two-by-four legs. Simply drape a cloth over the top, staple on a gathered skirt, and add a glass top if you wish. (Or use hook-and-loop tape to attach the skirt so it can be removed for easy cleaning.) Hang an interesting mirror over your vanity, add a bright lamp or makeup mirror and a bench or chair padded with matching fabric.

Yoli used this technique to create a distinctive vanity in a little alcove between the closets of her own bedroom. She simply hammered two pegs into the sides of the alcove and rested a board on them. She covered the board with a tiny black houndstooth check, stapled on a black-and-white polka-dot skirt, and draped more houndstooth fabric to cover the staples. A big black velvet bow decorates the center of the vanity, and an antique silver vanity set that has been in Yoli's family for three generations graces the top. On the wall behind, an onyx-and-nickel Art Deco mirror hangs beside a black wall sconce, while a high window, curtained in crisp white Battenburg lace, provides more light. The total effect is romantic yet restrained, the black-and-white color scheme adding drama and discipline to the ruffles and bows. This entire little grouping, which cost next to nothing, is one of Yoli's favorite creations.

A Window on Your World

Once you've furnished your beautiful bedroom, of course, you'll want to dress it with wonderful bed linens, curtains, and accessories. For linens, just head for your local discount store—they are full of fabulous patterns. Even better, find a closeout store or wait for a white sale. Coordinated sheet sets combine patterns beautifully—why not buy an extra set or two to make curtains and accessories?

Comforters and duvets are an easy and comfortable way to top your sheets and can be quickly recovered to match a change of decor. But old-fashioned chenille covers and dainty woven coverlets add a charming lightness to any room, especially one with old-fashioned furniture. Patchwork quilts are a perennial source of beauty and warmth, whether they cover the bed or hang on a wall. For a change, try weaving thin ribbon through the "holes" of a loosely woven thermal blanket and using that as a spread.

More often than not, it's the pillows on a bed that make it irresistible. Whether you like the luxury look of piled-up cushions or the more restrained appeal of simple pillow shams and perhaps a decorative pillow, make sure the pillows are puffy and comfortable. If you like to read in bed, you may enjoy a firmer pillow or bolster for support.

Whatever pillows you use, don't assume that they all have to match. You can combine pillowcases from your sheet sets, coordinating matching cases, and any other pillow covers that blend in. Antique white pillowcases with embroidered edges or crisp Battenburg lace covers top any bed happily. Or why not make throw pillows out of old chenille bedspreads and sew fringed curtain tiebacks to match?

*Perfume and incense
bring joy to the heart ...*

—The Book of Proverbs

For an interesting but subdued look, try dressing sheets, blankets, and pillows in layers of related solid colors—perhaps a dusty blue bottom sheet, a sage green top sheet, a soft yellow spread, and pillows covered in the same blue or green. Or layer your bed in warm pastels—yellow, apricot, and coral. You can even hang sheets for curtains in layers to match—outside panels of one color, inside panels in another, and tiebacks in the third shade.

A side note: If you do go for the piled pillows, think of where you can put the extra pillows while you sleep. A big basket, a trunk, or an open-armed chair near the bed can keep the spares off the floor but close at hand for making up the bed the next day.

Do you have one of those old-fashioned high beds that off-the-rack dust ruffles don't fit? For a price, you can order an extra-long ruffle from a specialty catalog. If you have basic sewing skills and a little time, you can make a ruffle fairly easily by attaching gathered strips of fabric to a fitted sheet. If you don't have the time, though, you can make a two-tiered ruffle for a full-sized bed by draping a full-sized ruffle on top of a king-sized one. The king-sized dust ruffle should reach to the floor while the full-sized ruffle covers the extra "decking" that shows on top. Another possibility is simply to tack fabric (perhaps an old tablecloth or bed-spread cut in strips) to the box spring and cover with a shorter dust ruffle.

Finishing Touches

How do you decorate the windows and the walls in your bedroom? The principles are the same here as anywhere in the house: use your imagination, and hang whatever you like. If you have a picture or object you really love, however, resist the temptation to hang it over your head in a place of honor. Instead, hang it on the wall opposite your feet so it greets you upon waking and says "good night" to you before you fall asleep.

Underfoot in a bedroom, you want a floor treatment that comforts your bare feet. In a cold climate, soft rugs and carpets will warm you. In a warm climate you might prefer bare wood, tile, marble, or even concrete. Pay close attention to the texture as well as the look. Whatever feels the best to your naked toes as you pad your way to the bathroom is what you want on your bedroom floor.

Don't forget the little touches that please the senses and calm the spirit. The bedroom is the perfect place for fragrant sachets, velvety scented oils, for sumptuous textures and soothing music.

And don't neglect your ceilings in this room where you spend so much of your time looking up. Paint the ceiling a contrasting shade, stencil the edges, even ask a friend for help and drape the whole ceiling like the inside of a tent. For a hint of starlight, stretch twinkle lights around the ceiling line and partially hide behind a strip of molding. Or even more simply, buy a packet of fluorescent stars from a toy store and create a constellation on your ceiling. The stars will soak up light during day and glow at night.

Day or night, with or without the stars, your bedroom should be your haven of joyful serenity. Whatever else you accomplish in a decorative sense, keep this peaceful picture foremost in your mind. Your bedroom should be furnished not only with what you need for sleeping and dressing, but also with whatever you need to refresh and renew your spirit. Focus your decorative efforts toward making it a place of beauty, of intimacy, of prayer . . . a beautiful chamber that brightens your days and sweetens your dreams.

Bright Ideas

Creating a Tablescape

To add interest to your dresser tops (or any flat surface in your home), try creating a tablescape. This is simply an artfully arranged still life featuring items that might otherwise jumble on top of the dresser. Group these necessary items along with lovely accents and vintage linens to create a pleasing group.

His dresser, for instance, could combine a little painted tray for pocket necessities, a glass holder with grandfather's watch, a hand-painted oil lamp, and a grouping of photos in silver frames.

Hers could feature an art nouveau statuette, a crystal vase full of antique hatpins, a round bowl of mixed flowers, and a silk scarf draped over the mirror. You could even leave one drawer partly open and arrange a pair of long gloves in the opening.

The effect, if you can pull it off, is to improve the view in your rooms by transforming a cluttered surface into a miniature work of art.

Kid Chic

Imaginative Living Spaces for Children

A PLACE TO PLAY, A PLACE TO SLEEP, a place to learn, a place to curl up and dream—a child's room is called upon to be all these things. In addition, it must be able to functionally store millions of small items while making it easy for a child to grow and change and learn to care for herself.

Sound like a big order? It is. Decorating a child's nursery or bedroom poses a set of unique challenges. Fortunately, it's also a lot of fun. Here is where you can express some of your wildest, most creative fantasies, indulging the child within you while providing rich stimulation for the child who lives with you. At the same time, you will have an unparalleled opportunity for teaching a child how to shape his or her own environment.

It's My Room

Where do you start in decorating a child's room? With the child! Unless she is an infant in arms, the young person (or persons) who is to occupy the room should have a say in what it will be like. Even a two-year-old can pick a favorite from among several colors or patterns. An older child can participate fully in gathering ideas, choosing a theme and a color scheme, shopping for furniture and fabric, paintings and papering. If possible, she should be the one to make most of the decisions (with you retaining veto power).

Not only is this fair, it's practical. The more input a child has in the decor of her own room, the more responsible she is likely to be in keeping that same room tidy. There's nothing like pride of ownership to encourage responsibility.

We ourselves have sometimes been astounded at how creative children can be when designing their own living space. Emilie's granddaughter, Christine, for example, designed a simple but truly unique space by stenciling the names of her friends in several colors on one wall. The other walls she painted in stripes of the same colors—and linens and drapes echoed this color scheme. The next year, of course, she had to repaint the "name wall" and change the names, but the expense was low and the effect was stunning.

We truly would never have thought of that—but we loved it when we saw it!

A Room for the Imagination

A truly wonderful child's room is both imaginatively designed and designed to stimulate the imagination. This is where the fun comes in. Try to provide a living space that encourages children to draw, paint, build, act, and create.

An easel set up near a window with a bucketful of crayons or chalk encourages daily works of art. So does an easily available lap desk or a small table and chairs. You can paint the back of the door with blackboard paint (available at hardware stores) or one wall with high-gloss enamel so the child can draw on the walls without fear of punishment. More simply, you can stretch rolls of white paper over a wall for impromptu mural making.

Children especially love cozy nooks where they can pretend they're in a house or cave or curl up to nap and enjoy a book. If you can, set aside a corner to create such a place. Drape fabric into a kind of awning, furnish a beanbag chair or some comfortable cushions, and add a basket for books, crayons, and toys. If you can't make space for such a nook on a permanent basis, show your child how to make a temporary cozy spot by draping a blanket over a card table. Or use fabric to curtain off the bed itself into a cozy hiding place.

One of the best ways to stimulate your child's imagination is to use your decorative skills to transform the room into a wonderful pretend environment. With some paint, some plywood or cardboard, and some imaginative props, your child's room can become a garden paradise complete with picket fence and flowers, a jungle full of animals, a beach hut, a romantic castle turret, or a tree house.

Don't be afraid to paint a scene or decoration directly on your child's wall. With a little paint you can create forests, gardens, menageries, whatever you

> *If you carry your childhood with you, you never become older.*
>
> —Abraham Sutzkever

wish. Don't worry too much about your artistic talents—a folk-art look only heightens the charm. But if you cannot bring yourself to work freehand, you still have many decorative options. Stencils or stamps are a great way to go. Fabric stores offer wonderful kid-patterned material, some suitable for framing or stapling to the wall. Or here's a great hint we learned from our friend Donna Otto: Borrow an opaque projector from your church or school and use it to project a pattern on the wall. Trace around the design with a pencil and simply follow the outline. This is a great way to transfer a design from a coloring book or children's book onto the wall of a child's room.

Decorating your child's room is truly a wonderful opportunity to shape her environment and shape her life. So use your imagination. Have fun. Make sure your child is involved. And don't worry that she will grow tired of the wonderful decor you create together. Remember that a child's room is supposed to change anyway!

When the time comes, simply enlist your child's help in setting another wonderful stage for imaginative living.

Bright Ideas

Eight Imaginative Themes
for Children's Bedrooms

✿ *Cowboys and Cowgirls.* Use rope for a curtain rod, bandanna print curtains, and a bed covered with denim and bandannas. An old book becomes a lamp, a ten-gallon hat decks the wall, and a horseshoe hangs over the door.

✿ *Circus Fantasy.* Paint walls and ceiling to resemble the inside of a circus tent—or hang tentlike fabric from the center of the ceiling. On one wall paint a mural of elephants or clowns. Curtain the windows in clown stripes and make a clown's-head pillow for the bed. Construct a "cage" along the wall to hold stuffed animals, and hang a "trapeze" from the ceiling to hold a doll.

✿ *The High Seas.* Have a little rowboat fitted with a custom mattress to make a bed. Paint a sail on the wall behind it or actually hang a piece of canvas diagonally across a corner. Paint or carpet the floor ocean blue, and continue the nautical theme around the room with anchors and life preservers.

☼ **On the Beach.** *Paint a little lighthouse or a tall palm tree on a wall. Hang a striped awning or a beach umbrella over the bed and put sisal mats on the floor. Curtain the windows with airy white and add a few plastic beach chairs.*

☼ **At the Theater.** *Build a sleeping platform or remove the bottom bunk from a set of bunk beds and create a miniature "stage" underneath. Hang a curtain, and stock a small trunk with costume material (old clothes, scarves, jewelry, and makeup). Also include a curtain panel that can be hung from two hooks halfway up to form a puppet stage. Continue the theater theme in the room with antique theater seats and movie posters.*

☼ **Tropical Paradise.** *A grass skirt from an import store becomes a bed ruffle and a surfer-print duvet cover continues the look. Old surfboards on brackets become shelves, ukuleles and leis decorate the walls, and Hawaiian-shirt fabric or fishnets form the curtains. A vintage Hawaiian lamp with a hula dancer, if you could find it, adds a whimsical touch.*

☼ **Tree House.** *In a corner, paint a tree trunk, then glue-gun silk leaves on walls and up onto the ceiling. Hang a little wooden swing from the ceiling. Set a doll or stuffed animal in the* swing. Be sure the child understands the swing is not for her—or attach it to a ceiling joist so she really can swing.

✿ **The Secret Garden.** Use picket fencing like wainscoting around a room and hang window boxes inside the windows with real or fake plants or flowers. Or if you have a closet that is not needed, create a wonderful "garden" inside by painting the walls. Use tall picketing for a backboard. Above the fence, paint the wall blue and sponge on white puffy "clouds."

16

Bathing Beauty

Wonder in the Washroom

WHERE CAN YOU GET the biggest return for the smallest decorating investment?

In the bath!

Not only are bathrooms great fun to decorate; their small area means they require less paint, less furniture, less time, and a lot less money to transform (assuming, of course, that you aren't planning to do any major tile or plumbing work!). And the payoff for creating a beautiful bathroom is surprisingly great for the small amount of time and money invested. After all, this is a room where you retire to be refreshed and rejuvenated. The decor you surround yourself with during these moments may well have a remarkable effect on your outlook during the rest of the day.

A Place to Experiment

Because your investment in bathroom decor is so small, it's a great place to experiment with decorating ideas. Don't be afraid of strong, rich colors—navy blue, rich red, even high-gloss yellow or glossy black. (But do check out how those colors affect the way you look in the mirror.) Experiment with unusual themes and fabrics you may not associate with bathrooms.

One of Yoli's favorite bathrooms, for instance, was a little service bath a friend designed. It features a black-and-white tile floor, yellow walls, vintage linens draped over a valance rod in the high, small window, and a cheerful bumblebee buzzing across the wall.

For another bathroom Yoli used denim fabric and red-and-white sailboat rope to create a casual nautical effect. Striped, monogrammed towels, a red-painted medicine cabinet, lighthouse pictures in funky frames, and a casual rag rug combined to complete the effect. The bathroom was cheerful and masculine, the total cost almost nothing.

With just a little ingenuity, you can create a bathroom that is fully as interesting or fun. Your bathroom can be gold and black, with an Egyptian theme, or pristine white in a variety of textures. You can paint the walls, paper them, decoupage them, or staple yards and yards of shirred fabric around them. (Be aware, however, that certain wall coverings may peel off in a steamy environment.)

Don't hesitate to hang pictures in your bathroom—not your treasured fine-art prints that might be damaged by steam and humidity, but plaques, posters, framed magazine covers, or even copies of treasured family photos. Mirrors and clocks are both naturals for bathrooms, but ceramic sculptures or silk flowers can also be wonderful. Try draping a garland of silk grape leaves around your big slab mirror or set an interesting bust atop a cement column in a corner.

Seashells also feel especially at home in a bathroom. You can set several shells in a bowl of potpourri or hang a group of giant starfish on a wall. Or glue shells to cover a picture frame, a tissue box, or even a chair rail.

Sue Casebeer, an inventive designer from Carbondale, Illinois, did this beautifully in her own bathroom. She simply painted a lattice strip, nailed it around the room as a chair rail, and covered it with an arrangement of shells, starfish, and sea horses. A shell-covered wreath and mirror frame pick up the motif, and the rest of the room is decorated in soft pink and peach tones that echo the color of the shells.

Lamps and candles are happy additions to any bathroom, no matter how well lit. A lamp on the counter adds an unmistakable note of warmth as well as an interesting accent—try one with a faceted crystal base and a shade created from a monogrammed hankie. Scented candles and potpourri sweeten the ambience as well as filling a more practical function.

Plants love bathrooms, too, and a bathroom full of plants can be especially refreshing. Hang them from the ceiling, line them up on windowsills, stack them on shelves in the corner. You can even string wires across the window and train ivy or other vines on the wires—an instant leafy window covering.

If you like the garden idea, in fact, it's an easy matter to turn your whole bathroom into a garden gazebo. Just cut latticework arches to cover a wall of soft green fading to blue. Hang plants from the points of the arches or center concrete columns under them to hold potted plants or garden statuary. Add a bench, a birdhouse, even a little bucket of garden tools. Paint ivy or morning glories twining up the lattice, and you'll think you're bathing in the garden of Eden! You can even stow your toothbrushes in a terra-cotta pot and stencil your shower curtain with leaves.

> *No room is too small to surround yourself with the accessories that turn daily routine into a celebration of pleasure.*
>
> —Alexandria Stoddard

If you love to luxuriate in the tub, be sure and decorate with those long soaks in mind. Tuck a little table near the tub to hold bubble bath, scented oils, and perhaps a magazine. And pay some attention to the ceiling you'll be looking up at. Paint it a lovely color, twine its edges with leafy stencils, or paint it navy blue and deck it with painted stars.

Fabric Finds

Shower curtains, window curtains, and sink skirts offer you an opportunity to decorate your bathroom beautifully with fabric. As long as you hang an inexpensive waterproof liner, almost any kind of fabric will work for a shower curtain. A tablecloth in cotton, vinyl, or even lace is often just the right size. Sheets can be trimmed and hemmed to size. (To hang, use a grommet punch or sew buttonholes to make openings for commercial rings. Or you can attach ribbons that tie directly to the rod.)

Washable window curtains in the appropriate size can also be used for your shower, and commercial shower curtains can be decorated by stamping, stenciling, or freehand painting. You can even use roll-up matchstick blinds from the import store for a truly unique shower curtain.

Because bathroom windows are usually small and often covered with opaque glass, curtains and shades can be simple and inexpensive. A simple valance, window scarf, or a set of lacy sheers may be all you need to add a lovely touch—perhaps with a set of miniblinds if you need the privacy. If you happen to have a window within the shower area, hand towels or dishtowels can make easy-care window coverings.

Basin skirts are time-honored but still effective devices for concealing ugly pipes under a sink and providing extra storage space as well. Making such a skirt is as easy as gathering hemmed strips of fabric (you can use iron-on shirring tape for this), gluing or sewing fabric to the "hook" side of hook-and-loop fastener tape, then hot-gluing the other side of the tape around the sink. For a more finished look, you can cover the gathered edge with ribbon, fabric trim, rope, or more draped fabric. Or vary the effect by pleating the skirt instead of gathering it.

More Quick Fixes

Skirts aren't the only tricks at your disposal for inexpensively handling unsightly or inadequate features in your bathroom. A worn iron bathtub can be painted on the outside with high-gloss enamel paint (and even decorated with a gold-paint pen); the inside can be reporcelained or just touched up with epoxy porcelain paint.

An unsightly bathroom cabinet can be spruced up by simply removing the doors and replacing them with a pretty curtain. Or remove the door panels, paint the cabinet, antique it with a crackling compound, and tack chicken wire in place of the door panels for the look of an antique pie safe.

If your bathroom has tile in a truly ugly color, you can paint over it with exterior-grade latex paint. We encourage you, however, to think carefully before you take such a step. In our experience, most tile adds a distinctive touch to a bathroom. With a little effort, you may be able to find a fabric or wallpaper that makes the tile work. Given a little time, you may even find you like it.

A shortage of towel racks is a problem in many bathrooms. If you need more—or you just don't like the ones you have—you can replace them in a moment with beautiful and inexpensive fixtures from your local hardware store. For a different look, however, try adding an antique quilt rack, a peg rail, or old-style brass hooks. Yoli uses large brass double hooks with porcelain knobs to hang bath linens in her own master bath. She hangs bath towels on the bottom hook and drapes some of her antique monogrammed linens over the top hook.

Lack of storage space is a problem in many bathrooms, one that can be solved with a little ingenuity. A pocketed shoe hanger on the back of a closet door is wonderful for storing everything from hair dryers to cotton swabs. A garage-sale wine rack can hold a collection of fluffy rolled-up towels; a white enamel bowl can humorously store a pile of white toilet paper rolls in an all-white bathroom. And if your bathroom counter is a clutter of miscellaneous bottles and tubes, simply buy a collection of interesting colored bottles and jars, pour your toiletries into these bottles, and label them on the bottom.

Bathroom Surprise

The most important thing to remember when decorating any bathroom is that you don't have to stick to the typical. Just a few unexpected touches can make your bathroom both beautiful and unique.

Paint designs on a few tiles behind your bathtub, for instance, or replace the handles on your cabinets with antique drawer pulls. And furnish your bath with items people might never expect, such as the glassed-in lawyers' bookcase that holds a collection of small items in Emilie's master bath or the little footstool that helps her in and out of her big iron tub.

There's nothing to say you can't hang a crystal chandelier in your elegant gold-and-white bathroom or put a birdbath filled with little soaps in your garden-themed one. An old-fashioned standing scale from a doctor's office or even a rusty wagon in the corner can add that unusual touch that makes a bathroom truly memorable. (Fill the wagon with magazines or towels or tuck in a potted plant.)

And don't forget the special comforting touches as well—an upholstered bench to sit on while undressing, a soft little rug underfoot, a basket of reading material, or a warming rack for towels. A fluffy robe hanging by a hook on the door is a comfort to guests, a decorative crock holding hand cream is a comfort to anybody. A funny or inspiring little gift book on a countertop adds to the feeling of welcome.

In the end, it is these little touches that represent the very best bathroom investment. Your purpose, after all, is not just to create a stunner of a room (though you want that, too). What you want is to design a space that leaves everyone feeling a little happier, a little more refreshed, a little more ready to face a new day or a comfortable night.

And that's not too much to ask, even for a little room full of plumbing.

Bright Ideas

Decorating with Mirrors—10 Great Ideas

Mirrors are wonderful decorating tools. They expand visual space and help you make the most of light as well as give you the opportunity to fix your face and check for spinach between your teeth. Here are some bright ideas for using mirrors in all your decorating schemes:

- ❀ Cut up a big slab of bathroom mirror, frame the pieces, and hang in an arrangement.

- ❀ Hang pictures directly on a large mirror using clear fishing wire attached to the ceiling molding. The pictures will appear to float in space.

- ❀ Hang an interesting empty frame over a large slab mirror.

- ❀ Buy inexpensive department-store mirrors, spray frames black, and gild with your gold-paint pen.

- ❀ Hang the mirror from an old dresser over a fireplace.

- ❀ Lean an interesting framed mirror inside a window to disguise a less-than-perfect view.

- ❀ Include framed mirrors in a wall arrangement.

✿ Always place a small mirror near the exit of your home for last-minute touch-ups.

✿ Use old mirror trays (designed for dressing tables), dime-store framed mirrors, or hardware-store mirror tiles as place mats.

✿ Glue-gun fabric ruffles around an oval mirror from the dime store and hang over a vanity with matching skirt.

17

Maintaining and Creating

The Case for Cute and Useful Work Spaces

FUNCTION AND BEAUTY are not mutually exclusive; they are two sides of the same decorating coin.

This is especially important to remember when you are decorating the rooms where you and others in your family do their work. We don't just mean home offices—though increasing numbers of people these days make their living from their homes. We also mean kitchens, which in addition to being the heartbeat of most homes, are also their preeminent work space. In the kitchen the daily necessities and creative expression of food preparation are taken care of. Many kitchens also serve as a kind of household central office—housing the main telephone, message center, and perhaps a small area for conducting household business.

Other household work spaces may include a utility room (if you are lucky enough to have one), a workshop or work area in a garage, a potting shed or gardening porch, and yes, any kind of study or home office. All these are areas for both maintaining and creating, and all are vital to a beautiful home.

Don't Neglect to Decorate

Any room where you work is a room where you need an extra dose of joy and motivation. These rooms in which you maintain and create should be the cheeriest in your home, filled with colors and objects that invigorate you, lift your spirit, and invite you to tackle the task at hand with enthusiasm. These should be rooms where you love to be.

And yet, with the possible exception of the kitchen and the study, these are the rooms that are often neglected in the task of decorating. These are the places where, without a little attention, mechanical function may quickly win out over beauty and inspiration.

You do need the function, of course. But you also need the beauty. So don't neglect to decorate your workrooms. Paint them in bright, invigorating colors or soothing, contemplative ones. Hide clutter in interesting boxes or baskets or behind drapes. And do deck the walls, even in the most homely work space. In many cases you can use your actual tools and supplies. A sewing corner, for instance, can catch the eye with a big supply of ribbons, remnants, and tools hanging from decorative hooks on the wall. An iron rack for hanging utensils or copper pots adds an easy, gleaming accent in a kitchen. Peg-Board in a utility room (or any room) can be very cheerful and decorative if you paint it a color that harmonizes with the room and then add contrasting outlines for the various items that you want to hang—from scissors to irons to art supplies.

These are also good rooms for whimsical decor, perhaps related to the function of the room. An office might hold a wall full of work-related cartoons or an inspiring quote rendered in beautiful calligraphy. Food and cooking themes as well as plates and other dishes are perennials for kitchens, and a framed pair of old laundry-soap advertisements can be adorable over your washing machine. A wall arrangement of outmoded tools can be highly amusing on the wall of a wood workshop. Offices and studies are often filled with books and "serious" accessories.

But don't limit yourself to topical decor. Anything that you find beautiful or interesting can find a decorative home in your workrooms.

A kitchen can be a home for a comfortable upholstered chair with a footstool (perfect for perusing recipes or resting on while something bakes). Its windowsill may hold a collection of miniature animals as well as a row of ripening tomatoes. An inspiring landscape or classic set of botanical prints can grace a wall, and a collection of family photos (copies to avoid damage from moisture and grease) or a gallery of framed children's art can cluster in a bright corner as well as on the refrigerator.

A sewing room, similarly, can sport a garden theme—complete with straw hats on the wall, garden paintings, or even latticework on the walls. An office wall can hold lighthearted movie posters or a collection of mugs as well as diplomas, plaques, and inspirational posters. And the more utilitarian work spaces, such as garages and utility rooms, are usually appreciative of any kind of decoration!

Emilie and her husband, Bob, are especially fond of the decor in their highly functional utility/sewing room. Besides the matching covers for the sewing machine and ironing board, stitched up by Emilie in an afternoon, the only real decorating is a wall of interesting pictures and plaques that were left over from decorating the rest of the house. These decorating "orphans," which both Bob and Emilie liked but just didn't have a place for, found a comfortable spot on the wall of their utility room. The gallery seems to grow with each new decorating effort, and the effect is infinitely more cheerful than a bare room with washer, dryer, ironing board, and work table.

Creative Equipping

Specialized work spaces need specialized equipment, and skimping on quality in certain items tends to be a poor bargain. Any piece of furniture or equipment you will use on a daily basis—from office chairs to task lights to file cabinets to chef's knives—should be the best you can afford. Pay special attention to ergonomic needs—a chair that supports your back, a desk or countertop that is the right height for the work you need to do, a saw or screwdriver that is sturdy and easy to grasp.

This doesn't, mean, however, that you always need to go with commercial or made-to-order solutions. With a little creativity, you may find less expensive and more interesting solutions and ideas for your specialized work space.

Many standard desks, for example, waste working space because they are too deep. You may do much better with a long, formica-covered countertop. These countertops are available in a variety of finishes from a home-repair center or hardware store. They are about 25 inches deep—as opposed to a yard or more for the average desk—and feature a curved lip that can fit down over a cabinet base or file cabinet. If you want, you can even have one cut to run the length of a wall. A smooth interior door or another large slab of wood can fill a similar purpose for a desk. Just pay attention to the proper heights for writing, key-boarding, and other work.

In the sewing room, on the other hand, you may find that the commercial sewing tables just don't give you enough space—perhaps a big, old desk from a thrift shop or a dinette table would suit you much better. Or try padding a large piece of plywood with several layers of blankets and cover with a bright sheet (wrap and staple underneath) for a combination ironing board/cutting table that rests on sawhorses or a smaller table during work sessions and that stands neatly behind a door when not needed.

The same combination of board and sawhorses can serve you as a laundry or craft table in the utility room or a work table in the garage. You can sand and paint it if you don't want to cover it with fabric—or you can staple a gathered fabric skirt to the edge to create an instant covered storage area.

Storage pieces, too, can be swapped between workrooms and borrowed from other rooms in your house. An armoire from the bedroom can hold office

If you want a golden rule that will fit everybody, this is it: Have nothing in your house that you do not know to be useful, or believe to be beautiful.

—William Morris

supplies or be fitted with glass shelves to become a china cabinet in the kitchen. A metal office cabinet (perhaps painted with an interesting mural or stamped with a geometric design) can stow soap and bleach in the laundry room or bolts of fabric in a sewing room. An old washstand, painted and distressed for an even more antique look, can hold your gardening pots and gloves and also serve as a work surface. An old wine rack from a garage sale might be just the thing you need to store rolled-up papers and plans, or a set of canisters from the kitchen might hold dog biscuits and supplies in another workroom.

Shelves and boxes from a variety of sources can serve you well in any workroom. Covered cardboard boxes perched on commercial utility shelves can be surprisingly attractive in a utility room or garage—but you can also hide them behind a bright canvas shade or a roll-up matchstick blind. Plastic crates stacked along one wall of a sewing room can organize supplies cheerfully; rest a long board on top for another display surface. Covered plastic kitchen organizers (from a home party or the grocery store) can beautifully hold anything from office supplies to gift wrap. Hatboxes or Shaker boxes from the craft store can store your working items efficiently—and wire bicycle baskets arranged on a wall can organize all manner of files and magazines.

Work Space Facelifts

Remember, too, that even utilitarian objects such as file cabinets, refrigerators, and built-in cabinetry can be refinished, painted, stained, and decorated. You don't have to be stuck with the look you started with.

Painting your appliances may well be a job you want to relegate to professionals, although you can do it yourself with special paint obtained from the manufacturer or service center. File cabinets, too, can be professionally painted, but they are not that hard to do yourself if you can manage to move them. Prime any rusted areas and simply spray with enamel. If you like, you can spray on several coats and then sand them gently for a burnished look.

Kitchen cabinets can also get a facelift from a simple coat of paint—or distress them, crackle them, stencil, or stamp them. You may choose to remove the cabinet doors entirely, replace them with glass-paneled doors, or hang little curtains to cover them. Paint and paper the cabinet interior, line the shelf edges with lace, add a little lamp, and let your stacks of crockery constitute your decor. If your time or budget won't allow that complete a change, try just replacing the handles—you'll be surprised at the difference such a small touch can make. Or just distract the eye from the cabinets with a beautiful potted plant in the window.

Do you know the best benefit that comes from decorating and revitalizing your work spaces?

The best thing is that you reap twice for a single sowing. First, you reap the joy of working in a wonderful room. Then, you reap the results of the creative and maintaining work you do there.

If your work spaces are cute and useful, you may even end up using them to decorate an ever more beautiful home.

18

Where Your Treasure Is

Decorating with Collections and Heirlooms

IT MAY OR MAY NOT BE TRUE that you are what you eat.

It is undeniably true, however, that you are what you love.

As a corollary, the things you love provide a mute but eloquent testimony to your interests and personality.

Your collection of Japanese fans. The bonnet and gloves you inherited from your great-grandmother. The teddy bears you've kept since childhood, and the pottery pieces your children have made—all of these may be treasures to you. And your personal treasures comprise your most revealing and often most effective decorating tool.

It's an important part of loving what you have—having the things you love on display as an integral part of your beautiful home.

How you do this, of course, will depend on what treasure you have accumulated. A giant collection of political campaign pins or a roomful of first-edition novels will pose a different decorating challenge than a beloved oil painting will. A collection of pennies in a jar will demand different treatment than a priceless Victorian wedding dress.

Many items, of course, will answer their own display questions. A collection of Christmas tree items should probably be displayed proudly on a tree during the holidays. (Though they may also be beautiful hanging from a wreath or a swag.) A favorite painting, similarly, will probably hang on the wall in a place of honor—but away from damaging sunlight and dust.

If your treasures are fragile or monetarily valuable, in fact, it's a good idea to invest in the hardware you need to display them properly. Glass-topped coffee tables and display cases can be quite appropriate for a treasured collection. Museum-quality framing techniques can protect watercolors and prints from dust, light, and acids. Special hangers for quilts and textiles can be purchased in quilting shops or through ads in quilting magazines.

But your options for displaying most of your treasures are certainly not limited to these kinds of "official" displays. Look up, down, and in corners for forgotten opportunities to display your special things. A plate rail might work above a window or around a small room. Extra shelves might fit nicely under the stairs or along a hallway. Perhaps your treasures could find a happy home on a bed or chair, on the floor, hanging on the wall, or even tucked into an unused fireplace.

Remodeled armoires, wardrobes, or even unused closets can make beautiful, functional display cases—just outfit with glass shelves and add display lights if necessary. Emilie's treasured teacup collection has long lived in such an armoire. Old store fixtures (sewing displays, glove racks, and so forth) make unique and interesting collection cases. Look for these at flea markets and antique stores, or check the want ads for stores that are going out of business.

Don't overlook hooks and hangers for displaying textiles and other small items. An antique christening dress or a collection of old vests can be beautifully displayed on velvet-covered hangers around a room. And quilts and coverlets don't have to be stretched out on a bed or on a wall. Try stacking them on a shelf or under a table so that the colorful patterns show.

Small groups of related treasures can be especially effective when grouped together in a little vignette on a tablet or bureau. Your beloved family Bible draws the eye more quickly when it is arranged in an artful still life with a dainty china teacup and a pair of old, wire-rimmed eyeglasses. A pair of antique gloves gains interest when displayed with a guest book, an antique pen, and a silver-and-crystal inkwell.

A variant to this kind of vignette that might work better with fragile treasures is the shadow box. A Victorian bonnet, a feathered fan, an embroidered hankie, and a beautiful beaded purse are all lovely in their own right, but grouping them together under glass both preserves them and displays them in an unforgettable way. The same technique could display your wedding invitation, silk bouquet, and garter. Shadow boxes are not hard to find in craft stores and frame shops, along with a variety of small hanging cabinets that will beautifully house a group of small treasures.

For where your treasure is, there your heart will be also.

—The Book of Matthew

Collections pose a special challenge when it comes to decorating. How do you show off your lovingly gathered multiple treasures in a way that displays them to advantage and invites conversation without cluttering the house and overwhelming the decor?

We've found that it usually works best to group collections together rather than scattering them willynilly around the house. A herd of miniature rocking horses galloping across a plate rail or a flock of clocks clustered on the mantel will be far more appealing than lonely individual items stationed around your house. And your grandma's hand-crocheted doilies will be far more effective tacked onto a group of pillows or draped over a valance rod than frosting every chair or sofa in the house. The collection itself, in other words, becomes a decorating item, not the individual pieces.

Grouping your collections, however, doesn't necessarily mean you must always cluster them in one corner or one set of shelves. You might find it more effective to let your collection set the theme for a room and let individual items around the room carry the theme.

If you collect elephant statues, for instance, you might decide to let your den become an "elephant room." A sizable wooden elephant from India could hold up a piece of glass for a coffee table. A parade of smaller pachyderms could march across a windowsill, while your bronze elephant bookends hold some books about elephants. A cluster of other miniature elephants could live on the bookends.

Similarly, your pieces of pink Depression glass might tie a room together by providing a color motif that shows up in several corners. Or if you collect cookie jars, you might line up your favorites across the mantel but turn one or two into table decorations or even lamps.

If the items in your collection are small, however, it's almost always advisable to mass them together to give them more visual weight. Crowd small toys together on a table or gather your collection of tiny glass jars on a mirror or tray. Type trays from old printing establishments and wooden beverage cases have long been popular for displaying miniature collectibles, and wall-hung cabinets and shelves are naturals for this kind of display. Other possibilities include baskets, muffin tins, open drawers, or shadow boxes.

Have you ever thought of your family photos as a collection? (You know, of course, that they are a treasure!) Because photos come in such a wide variety—candids and formal shots, color and black and white, expensive studio frames and cheap dime-store frames—you might consider grouping photos that have at least something in common.

One of Emilie's tables, for instance, holds photos of the women in her family. The shots cover several generations and are displayed in a variety of frames, but the mother-daughter-granddaughter motif pulls the collection together and invites the interest of passersby.

There are many ways to provide this "same but different" effect with a group of photographs.

You can group all black-and-white photos in a miscellany of frames, or group color, black-and-white, formal, and informal in identical frames. Yet another idea is to keep the same frames on your tables or walls but change the photos seasonally—Christmas pictures at Christmas, colored-leaf shots in the fall, beach pictures in the summer.

What do you do if you have a large collection and nowhere to display it? One strategy might be to store most of it and rotate specific items in and out of a small display case. Another possibility is to build a special display or even a room for your collection—although that may move us beyond the idea of decorating on a budget.

Whenever you are displaying a collection or grouping any like items together, remember the principle of staging a surprise. Make sure there's always a "dysfunctional element"—a designer's term for one that adds quirk and character to a display by being just a little different. Thus a tall coffeepot might nest among your flock of squatty teapots, or an overturned teacup might disturb your row of primly upright ones. Tuck an artichoke in a bowl of apples, a white folk-art sheep in a herd of black ones, a red high-top sneaker in row of vintage high heels. There's nothing like the minor shock of a dysfunctional element to draw the eye and inspire a smile.

And that, of course, is what you want whenever you decorate with your treasured possessions. You want to attract attention, start conversations, share the objects you love with others.

It's just another form of sharing yourself. And sharing yourself, again, is an important part of decorating your beautiful home.

Bright Ideas

Collections You Might Not Know You Have
(And How to Turn Them into Decorating Gold)

- ✿ Hand-me-down treasures from a favorite relative (an old hymnbook, a church fan, a Scripture bookmark, and a childhood photo). Display by grouping in an interesting vignette or hang in a shadow box frame.

- ✿ Knitting needles and skeins of yarn. Collect in open boxes or baskets, or display needles in a tall vase.

- ✿ Baskets. Hang in a group on wall or from ceiling, or cluster under a side table.

- ✿ Evening bags. Hang as a wall grouping or in a shadow box.

- ✿ Scarves. Drape around mirrors, use as valances or wall hangings.

- ✿ Pictures with a related theme (animals, plants, colors). Hang together in a symmetrical or unsymmetrical group.

- ✿ Travel mementos. Display on shelves or in a glass case, or frame for wall display.

❀ Old books. Line up on shelves or stack on tables.

❀ Painted trays. Use as tabletops or display on walls.

❀ Dishes with similar designs or color (including your china pattern). Display in china cabinets, on plate rails, or with plate hangers on the wall; or arrange on an antique sideboard.

❀ Costume jewelry. Hang interesting pieces on velvet or a length of lace, or arrange in a display case.

❀ Cookbooks. Paint a funky little bookcase for the kitchen and line them up in easy reach.

19

Make Your Clutter Cute

♡

Inspired Solutions for Your Decorating Dilemmas

FOR MANY OF US, the majority of our decorating problems can be filed under one heading: stuff. Quite simply, we have too much of it. Stuff fills our lives. We don't know where to put it. We don't know how to hide it. Or we don't know how to use it.

How do you solve the problems of storage and disguise that sometimes leave you scratching your head? Try one of these all-purpose strategies.

Screen It

A beautiful decorated screen can effectively cover a multitude of decorating "sins," from an unsightly rowing machine to an extra hanging rack for your out-of-season clothes. In addition, a screen can be a decorative item in its own right, whether it is painted, covered with fabric, or shaped.

Almost any technique you use to decorate a wall can decorate a screen. You can paint it, texture it, antique it, pad and upholster it. A screen painted to match the walls becomes an almost invisible part of the architecture. A screen hand-painted with a brilliant mural, on the other hand, can step out to become a room's focal point.

Screens can be almost any size. Why not construct a three-foot screen with whimsical stenciling to give the kitty a bit of privacy in her litter box, or a four-foot lattice screen to disguise the radiator? Or decorate a half-size screen to partition off a special "reading corner" for your children in a large family room.

When considering screens to disguise your decorating eyesores, don't forget that furniture can sometimes serve the same purpose. An armoire placed at an angle across a corner creates an instant storage space for little-used items. A bookcase standing out from the wall instead of against it can define a small alcove for storage or other purposes. Any piece of large furniture pulled out just slightly from the wall can create a narrow niche for storing a card table.

Box It

A set of matching or attractive boxes or baskets provides instant and attractive storage for awkward items. If the box looks good, there's no reason you can't keep it right out in the open.

Emilie has long been famous for covering standard office-size cardboard boxes with paper or fabric and trim; everything from games to magazines to office supplies live happily in these instant trunks. Hatboxes,

Shaker boxes, picnic baskets, antique trunks—any kind of attractive container—can serve the same purpose of storing items you need but don't want to leave out in the open.

Make It Cute

A little imagination can transform many small objects into decorative items. Try tucking them into open baskets, gathering them into matched jars, hanging them in boxes or bags. Use paint, trim, and creativity to transform a potential eyesore or utility item into a beautiful or whimsical part of your decor.

Instead of just leaving the dog's dish in a corner, for example, why not transform the dog's dining area into a humorous focal point? Yoli did this for one client by painting the end of one of her cabinets green, adding a little doghouse with the dog's name over the door. In front she put a little place mat with the dog's food and water bowl. In another house Yoli found a pair of framed prints featuring dogs and hung them low on the wall just above the dog's dishes.

Get Rid of It

This is always an important option, especially with items that clutter up your house and distract from your beautiful decor. Periodically inspect the contents of your home with an eye for "Do I really need this?" You might even consider going through each closet and each room a little at a time (Emilie recommends doing it 15 minutes a day!) making decisions about what you want to keep and what can go.

When an item has served its purpose in your home, it may well be ready for charity or the dumpster. Better yet, send it to a consignment shop, take it to a swap meet, or have a garage sale—and use the proceeds for more decorating treasure.

Bright Ideas

A Storehouse of Quick Storage Ideas

☼ Use spray adhesive to cover a cardboard box with fabric; add trim and use in any room of the house.

☼ Store rolled-up towels in a garage-sale wine rack, an enameled washtub, or a wire bike basket attached to the wall.

☼ Install a shelf about a foot from the ceiling in a small room; use to store pitchers, punch bowls, and other large, attractive, but seldom-used items.

☼ Paint a metal utility cabinet or metal utility shelves in bright colors and use in a child's room. Old school lockers are also wonderful.

☼ Remodel your closet with vinyl-covered metal shelving.

☼ Hang Peg-Board in your kitchen for utensils and pots, outline each with a bold color to maintain the design when the item is being used and to remind you where to replace it.

☼ Replace a chair rail or wainscoting with a Shaker-style peg rail. Hang with vintage clothing.

- ✿ *Install a row of gleaming brass hooks in a corner.*

- ✿ *Paint a child's unfinished toy box in adult colors and use as a lamp table with lots of storage.*

- ✿ *Hang all your baskets on one wall and use them to hold your napkins and table linens.*

- ✿ *Assemble a collection of baskets, tackle boxes, toolboxes in various sizes; paint in coordinating colors and line up across a row of bookshelves.*

- ✿ *Refinish an old chest of drawers to hold videotapes or CDs.*

- ✿ *Locate a used card catalog (from a library that is computerizing its records) to store audiotapes.*

A Final Word

IN THE END, WHAT REALLY MATTERS is the sharing.

You want your house beautiful (even on a budget).

You want it comfortable and cozy for you and your family.

But whatever you do to your walls and your windows, don't forget that the most wonderful adornment to your home is your spirit of hospitality, your willingness to share your home and your lives with others.

You don't need to wait until everything's perfect. It will never be. After all, people live in your house. Something will always need painting or recovering or replacing. You'll always be wanting to add something here, take out something there.

But share anyway. Love what you have and invite others in to share the bounty. Your gracious welcome will fill the gaps and make the problems seem to disappear.

Your home will always be its most beautiful when you stretch out your arms in welcome and say, as Yoli's sweet, gracious grandmother always said,

"Mi casa es su casa."

To obtain information about
Emilie Barnes' seminars, tapes,
and other helpful time-management
products, send a self-addressed,
stamped envelope to:

More Hours in My Day
2838 Rumsey Drive
Riverside, California 92506

Other Books by
Emilie Barnes

Welcome Home

Let your home express your love and hospitality. Learn how to make a cozy first impression, prepare a chamber of romance, and create your dream home on a creative budget. View these ideas in action with photographs by Mark Lohman, who also captured the pure charm of Emilie's home in *Better Homes and Gardens*.

Simply Organized

Discover easy ways to sort through the paper pile, ideas to give you more hours in your day, and surefire strategies to get your family involved.

If Teacups Could Talk

This charmingly illustrated book combines colorful vignettes from the history of English teatime with practical ideas for extending hospitality. Includes directions for making perfect tea and recipes for favorite teatime foods.

Timeless Treasures

Exquisitely designed with the romantic artwork of Sandy Lynham Clough, *Timeless Treasures* offers warm vignettes on collecting and displaying family heirlooms, giving thoughtful gifts, and leaving treasures for coming generations.

Time Began in a Garden

An inspiring look at at the pleasures of God's garden gifts, *Time Began in a Garden* is filled with quotations and Scripture. The garden springs to life in this delightfully illustrated book.

Other Books by
Emilie Barnes

Christmas Is Coming
Let's Have a Tea Party
The Very Best Christmas Ever!
A Little Book of Manners
Simply Dinner
Treasured Christmas Memories

Dear Reader:

We would appreciate hearing from you regarding *Decorating Dreams on a Budget*. It will enable us to continue to give you the best in Christian publishing.

1. What influenced you to purchase this book?

   ❑ Author
   ❑ Subject matter
   ❑ Backcover copy
   ❑ Recommendations
   ❑ Cover/Title
   ❑ Other_____

2. Where did you purchase this book?

   ❑ Christian bookstore
   ❑ General bookstore
   ❑ Department store
   ❑ Grocery store
   ❑ Other_____

3. Your overall rating of this book:

   ❑ Excellent ❑ Very good ❑ Good ❑ Fair ❑ Poor

4. How likely would you be to purchase other books by this author?

   ❑ Very likely ❑ Somewhat likely ❑ Not very likely ❑ Not at all

5. What types of books most interest you? (check all that apply.)

   ❑ Women's books
   ❑ Marriage books
   ❑ Current Issues
   ❑ Christian Living
   ❑ Bible Studies
   ❑ Fiction
   ❑ Biographies
   ❑ Children's books
   ❑ Youth books
   ❑ Other_____

6. Please check the box next to your age group.

   ❑ Under 18 ❑ 18-24 ❑ 25-34 ❑ 35-44 ❑ 45-54 ❑ 55 and over

Mail to:
Editorial Director
Harvest House Publishers
1075 Arrowsmith
Eugene, OR 97402

Name _____

Address _____

State _____ Zip _____

Thank you for helping us to help you in future publications!